MQTT: Lightweight Messaging for the Internet of Things

James Relington

DEDICATION

To those who seek knowledge, inspiration, and new perspectives—
may this book be a companion on your journey, a spark for curiosity,
and a reminder that every page turned is a step toward discovery.

AKNOWLEDGEMENTS

I would like to express my deepest gratitude to everyone who contributed to the creation of this book. To my colleagues and mentors, your insights and expertise have been invaluable. A special thank you to my family and friends for their unwavering support and encouragement throughout this journey.

Introduction to MQTT and IoT

The Internet of Things, commonly abbreviated as IoT, has transformed the way devices, systems, and even entire industries communicate and operate. At its core, IoT refers to the network of interconnected devices embedded with sensors, software, and other technologies that allow them to collect and exchange data over the Internet. These devices can range from small, simple sensors in a smart home to complex machinery on factory floors or entire fleets of connected vehicles. As the IoT landscape continues to expand, with billions of devices now connected globally, the need for efficient, lightweight, and reliable communication protocols has become increasingly important. This is where MQTT, which stands for Message Queuing Telemetry Transport, comes into play as a vital component of the IoT ecosystem.

MQTT is a lightweight, publish-subscribe network protocol designed to transport messages between devices and servers with minimal overhead. Originally developed in the late 1990s by IBM, MQTT was created to address the need for reliable communication in environments where bandwidth is limited, network conditions are unreliable, and processing power is constrained. Its design philosophy was simple: create a protocol that is easy to implement, consumes low power, and can operate effectively in situations where other protocols might fail. MQTT has since gained widespread adoption across a variety of industries and applications, becoming one of the most popular protocols used in IoT deployments today.

One of the key reasons MQTT is so well-suited for IoT is its minimal footprint. Unlike traditional communication protocols that can be verbose and resource-intensive, MQTT operates with very small message headers and requires minimal network bandwidth. This makes it an ideal choice for IoT devices, many of which are battery-powered or operate in remote locations with intermittent connectivity. By reducing the amount of data transmitted and optimizing how devices communicate with servers or brokers, MQTT helps extend device battery life and reduce operational costs.

The publish-subscribe model employed by MQTT is another factor that contributes to its efficiency and scalability. In this model, devices known as publishers send messages to a central server called a broker, which then distributes those messages to devices known as subscribers. Publishers and subscribers do not communicate with each other directly; instead, they rely on the broker to manage and route messages based on topics. Topics are essentially message channels that help organize the data and determine which devices receive specific information. This decoupling of publishers and subscribers allows MQTT to support dynamic, flexible communication patterns where devices can join or leave the network without disrupting the entire system.

MQTT is also designed to be highly reliable, offering different levels of Quality of Service (QoS) that determine how messages are delivered. Devices and applications can choose the appropriate QoS level based on their specific requirements, balancing between message delivery assurance and network resource consumption. This feature is critical for IoT scenarios where losing data might not be acceptable, such as in healthcare monitoring systems or industrial automation processes. On the other hand, applications that prioritize speed and efficiency over guaranteed delivery, like environmental sensors reporting non-critical data, can opt for lower QoS levels.

Security is another important aspect of MQTT, especially as IoT systems often handle sensitive data or control critical infrastructure. Although the core MQTT protocol does not define built-in security mechanisms, it is commonly deployed alongside encryption protocols such as TLS (Transport Layer Security) and authentication mechanisms like username-password or certificate-based systems. This layered approach to security helps ensure that data transmitted over MQTT remains confidential, tamper-proof, and accessible only to authorized devices and users.

In recent years, the widespread use of MQTT has been accelerated by the growth of cloud computing and edge computing paradigms. Cloud platforms offer scalable MQTT broker services that make it easier for businesses and developers to deploy IoT solutions without managing physical servers. At the same time, the rise of edge computing has brought MQTT to devices operating closer to the data source, reducing latency and improving system responsiveness. This flexibility allows MQTT to be used across a wide variety of IoT architectures, whether cloud-based, edge-based, or hybrid.

MQTT's adaptability has also led to its adoption in diverse industries beyond traditional IoT sectors. In agriculture, farmers use MQTT to connect soil sensors, weather stations, and irrigation systems to optimize crop yields. In transportation, connected vehicles rely on MQTT to report location data, diagnostics, and safety information in real time. In smart homes, MQTT underpins the seamless communication between lighting systems, thermostats, and security devices. Even financial services and energy management companies have found innovative ways to leverage MQTT's efficiency and reliability in their digital ecosystems.

As the IoT landscape continues to evolve, MQTT's role as a foundational communication protocol is becoming increasingly significant. Its simplicity, robustness, and versatility enable developers to create highly responsive and resilient systems that can operate in a variety of environments, from urban centers to remote rural areas. Whether it's enabling smart cities, automating industrial processes, or powering consumer IoT products, MQTT has proven to be a crucial enabler of the connected world we live in today. With billions of IoT devices expected to come online in the coming years, understanding and leveraging MQTT will remain essential for anyone working in or around the IoT space.

The Evolution of IoT Communication Protocols

The journey of communication protocols within the Internet of Things (IoT) has been marked by continuous innovation, driven by the exponential growth of connected devices and the unique demands of various industries. In the earliest stages of machine-to-machine (M2M) communication, proprietary and specialized protocols were often used to allow devices to exchange information. These early systems were typically closed, designed for specific hardware or industrial environments, and lacked interoperability with other networks or platforms. The need for devices to communicate in isolated environments without the internet led to custom-built solutions that were expensive to maintain and difficult to scale.

As the concept of IoT began to take shape, a shift toward open and standardized protocols became necessary. The proliferation of sensors, actuators, and smart devices highlighted the importance of having protocols that could operate across diverse hardware and software environments. Early adaptations of existing internet technologies were applied to IoT, with protocols such as HTTP and FTP being repurposed to enable device communication over IP networks. However, these protocols were not designed for the constraints of IoT devices, many of which operate with limited power, memory, and processing capabilities. HTTP, for example, is a stateless, request-response protocol that is relatively heavy due to its verbose headers and reliance on TCP connections, making it suboptimal for battery-powered or bandwidth-limited devices.

Recognizing these limitations, engineers and researchers began developing protocols specifically tailored for IoT applications. One significant milestone in this evolution was the introduction of the Message Queuing Telemetry Transport (MQTT) protocol. MQTT's lightweight design, low power consumption, and publish-subscribe messaging model made it an ideal solution for many IoT scenarios. Its ability to function effectively over unreliable networks with constrained bandwidth allowed MQTT to quickly gain traction, particularly in industrial automation, transportation, and remote monitoring applications. MQTT's success underscored the growing trend toward protocols that prioritize efficiency and reliability in resource-constrained environments.

Around the same time, other protocols emerged to address different IoT use cases. The Constrained Application Protocol (CoAP) was developed as a lightweight alternative to HTTP, specifically designed to run over UDP instead of TCP. CoAP supports request-response interactions like HTTP but with a much smaller footprint, making it better suited for constrained devices and lossy networks. CoAP also introduced mechanisms for multicast communication, which is beneficial in scenarios where a single device needs to communicate with multiple nodes simultaneously, such as in smart lighting systems or sensor networks.

In parallel, protocols like Advanced Message Queuing Protocol (AMQP) and Extensible Messaging and Presence Protocol (XMPP) were adapted for IoT applications. AMQP, originally designed for financial services and enterprise messaging, provided a more feature-rich alternative with advanced queuing, routing, and reliability capabilities. However, its complexity and heavier overhead limited its adoption to specific IoT use cases that required robust message brokering and transactional reliability. XMPP, on the other hand, originally intended for instant messaging, introduced extensibility and real-time communication features that found niche applications in IoT, particularly in social and collaborative systems.

The evolution of IoT communication protocols did not stop with MQTT, CoAP, AMQP, or XMPP. As IoT expanded into more critical and large-scale domains, new hybrid and specialized protocols began to emerge. One such development was MQTT-SN (MQTT for Sensor Networks), a variant of MQTT tailored for wireless sensor networks and other non-IP environments. By reducing protocol overhead even further and incorporating support for simpler transport mechanisms, MQTT-SN enabled highly constrained devices to participate in publish-subscribe networks without the need for full IP stacks.

With the growth of edge computing and fog computing architectures, the requirements for IoT communication also evolved. Devices now needed to communicate not only with centralized cloud servers but also with local edge nodes capable of processing data closer to the source. This shift led to the adaptation and integration of protocols across different layers of the network. For instance, systems might combine MQTT for device-to-gateway communication with HTTP or gRPC for gateway-to-cloud interactions. This layered approach helped address latency concerns, reduce bandwidth consumption, and enhance the overall responsiveness of IoT solutions.

Another major factor influencing the evolution of IoT communication protocols has been the emergence of low-power wide-area networks (LPWANs) such as LoRaWAN, Sigfox, and NB-IoT. These networks enable devices to transmit small amounts of data over long distances while consuming minimal power. While LPWAN technologies are not protocols themselves, they necessitated the development of application layer protocols that could operate efficiently over low-data-rate links. Protocols like CoAP and lightweight custom protocols have been adapted to work within these constrained environments, enabling remote sensors and devices to report data over kilometers with battery lifespans measured in years.

Security considerations have also played a critical role in shaping IoT communication protocols. As devices became interconnected on a massive scale, concerns about data privacy, integrity, and authentication became paramount. Modern IoT protocols now incorporate or integrate with security layers such as Transport Layer Security (TLS), Datagram Transport Layer Security (DTLS), and Public Key Infrastructure (PKI) systems. This has led to a balance between maintaining lightweight designs while ensuring that sensitive data and critical infrastructure are protected from cyber threats.

Today, the landscape of IoT communication protocols is characterized by a diverse ecosystem, each protocol serving specific niches and technical requirements. From home automation to industrial control systems, smart cities to wearable health devices, the evolution of protocols has empowered IoT to penetrate every corner of modern life. The growing interoperability between these protocols, facilitated by middleware and IoT platforms, has made it possible to integrate devices and systems that once operated in silos.

The rapid advancement of technologies such as 5G, artificial intelligence, and blockchain will continue to influence how IoT devices communicate in the future. The need for ultra-reliable, low-latency communication will drive further protocol innovation, while edge-native and AI-powered devices will push for even more optimized communication patterns. This continuous evolution underscores the vital role that communication protocols play in shaping the future of IoT, creating a world where billions of devices seamlessly share information to drive smarter, more efficient, and more responsive systems.

Why MQTT? Key Features and Benefits

As the Internet of Things continues to expand into nearly every industry and sector, the demand for an efficient, reliable, and adaptable messaging protocol has never been greater. Amid the array of protocols designed to facilitate machine-to-machine communication, MQTT stands out as one of the most popular and widely adopted solutions. Its success lies in its ability to meet the unique demands of IoT environments, where devices are often constrained in terms of processing power, battery life, and network bandwidth. MQTT is purpose-built to address these challenges, offering a set of features and benefits that make it the protocol of choice for countless IoT applications around the world.

One of the most compelling reasons to choose MQTT is its exceptionally lightweight design. Unlike traditional internet protocols that rely on large, complex headers and verbose data structures, MQTT minimizes overhead by using compact message formats. This characteristic is critical in IoT ecosystems, where devices frequently operate with limited memory, CPU resources, and intermittent or unreliable network connections. By transmitting messages with as little as two bytes of fixed header information, MQTT enables even the simplest microcontrollers to participate in efficient and responsive communication networks. The reduced overhead not only conserves device power but also reduces operational costs by limiting bandwidth consumption.

Another major benefit of MQTT is its publish-subscribe architecture, which introduces flexibility and scalability to IoT systems. In this model, devices classified as publishers send messages to an intermediary known as a broker, which in turn distributes those messages to interested subscribers. This decoupling of message producers and consumers allows devices to communicate without having direct knowledge of one another, making system design more modular and adaptable. As IoT networks scale up and evolve, new devices can be easily integrated without the need for reconfiguring existing connections. This attribute is particularly valuable in large-scale deployments, such as smart cities or industrial environments, where thousands or even millions of devices might need to seamlessly share data.

The topic-based filtering mechanism of MQTT further enhances its ability to manage communication in complex networks. By organizing messages into hierarchical topics, MQTT allows subscribers to receive only the information relevant to them. This filtering system reduces unnecessary data transmission, thereby optimizing both network efficiency and device processing loads. For example, in a smart agriculture deployment, temperature sensors can publish to a specific topic like farm1/fieldA/temperature, while soil moisture sensors publish to a different topic such as farm1/fieldA/moisture. Devices or applications only interested in specific types of data can subscribe to the relevant topics, eliminating the need to process extraneous messages.

Reliability is another cornerstone of MQTT's design, supported by its built-in Quality of Service (QoS) levels. The protocol offers three distinct QoS levels to accommodate different application requirements. The first level, QoS 0, delivers messages on a best-effort basis without requiring acknowledgments. This is suitable for scenarios where occasional data loss is tolerable. QoS 1 ensures that messages are delivered at least once, providing a balance between reliability and efficiency. For applications where guaranteed delivery is paramount, QoS 2 delivers messages exactly once by employing a two-step handshake process. This granular control over message delivery is critical in IoT environments where varying levels of reliability may be necessary depending on the specific use case.

In addition to its lightweight and reliable nature, MQTT excels in environments characterized by unstable or unreliable network connectivity. IoT devices deployed in remote or challenging locations, such as offshore oil platforms or rural farmlands, often face intermittent network availability. MQTT's session persistence and automatic reconnect capabilities help devices resume communication quickly after disconnections, without requiring complex recovery logic. The Last Will and Testament feature further adds resilience by allowing devices to predefine a message that is broadcast by the broker in case of unexpected device disconnection. This mechanism is invaluable for monitoring device health and maintaining the integrity of distributed IoT networks.

Security is also a key factor in MQTT's widespread adoption. Although the core MQTT specification does not mandate security features, it is commonly paired with robust encryption and authentication mechanisms such as TLS for securing data in transit and username-password or certificate-based schemes for verifying client identities. This layered approach enables MQTT to be implemented in security-conscious environments where protecting data privacy and ensuring the authenticity of devices is non-negotiable. Organizations deploying MQTT-based systems can take advantage of established security practices while tailoring the implementation to meet their specific regulatory and operational requirements.

Another advantage of MQTT is its versatility across different types of networks and deployment models. MQTT can be used over standard TCP/IP networks, making it compatible with traditional internet infrastructure, but it can also be adapted to run over WebSockets, enabling easy integration with web applications and browser-based clients. Additionally, MQTT's suitability for edge computing scenarios has made it a critical component in distributed IoT systems. Devices can publish data to local edge servers or gateways running MQTT brokers, which process and analyze information locally before forwarding only relevant insights to centralized cloud systems. This reduces latency, optimizes bandwidth utilization, and enhances system responsiveness—key benefits for mission-critical applications such as autonomous vehicles or smart manufacturing lines.

The availability of MQTT client libraries in virtually every major programming language, including Python, Java, C, C++, JavaScript, and Go, has made it accessible to a broad range of developers. Open-source MQTT brokers such as Eclipse Mosquitto, as well as commercial brokers provided by major cloud platforms like AWS IoT Core, Microsoft Azure IoT Hub, and Google Cloud IoT Core, further contribute to its widespread adoption. This broad ecosystem ensures that MQTT can be easily integrated into existing workflows, making it easier for organizations to develop, deploy, and maintain IoT solutions without reinventing the wheel.

Ultimately, MQTT's combination of low resource consumption, reliable message delivery, flexible publish-subscribe architecture, and security extensibility positions it as a protocol uniquely suited to the demands of modern IoT networks. Its ability to bridge the gap between resource-constrained devices and powerful cloud services has made it indispensable in a world where billions of connected devices must operate efficiently, securely, and at scale. As IoT technologies continue to advance, the role of MQTT as a backbone for lightweight, scalable communication is set to remain as crucial as ever.

MQTT Architecture Overview

The architecture of MQTT is a cornerstone of its success in enabling efficient and reliable communication in the Internet of Things. Built around the publish-subscribe paradigm, MQTT's architecture is designed to facilitate lightweight messaging between devices while remaining simple to implement and highly scalable. Its core components—clients, the broker, and topics—work together to create a dynamic and flexible communication infrastructure that can support everything from a few devices in a smart home to millions of connected endpoints in a global IoT deployment.

At the heart of the MQTT architecture is the broker, a centralized server that acts as the intermediary between all connected clients. Unlike traditional client-server architectures where devices communicate directly with each other, MQTT clients never communicate peer-to-peer. Instead, all interactions are mediated through the broker, which is responsible for receiving messages from publishers and forwarding them to the appropriate subscribers based on topic subscriptions. This centralization simplifies system design by decoupling devices, making it unnecessary for publishers to know the identity or address of subscribers, and vice versa. The broker manages all message routing, topic matching, and client session persistence, reducing the burden on individual devices.

MQTT clients, which can be either publishers or subscribers—or both—are devices or applications that connect to the broker to send or receive messages. A publisher sends data to the broker on specific topics, while a subscriber expresses interest in receiving messages from specific topics by subscribing to them. The decoupled nature of MQTT clients means that devices can be dynamically added or removed from the network without impacting the overall system. A temperature sensor in a greenhouse, for example, might publish temperature readings to a broker under a topic like greenhouse1/temperature. At the same time, a separate monitoring application or an automated ventilation system subscribes to the same topic to receive these updates and act accordingly.

The concept of topics is critical to how MQTT organizes and routes messages. Topics in MQTT are strings that create a hierarchical structure, usually separated by forward slashes. This hierarchy allows for flexible message filtering and easy organization of data streams. For instance, in a smart building, topics could be structured as building1/floor2/room5/temperature, building1/floor2/room5/humidity, and so forth. Subscribers can leverage wildcards to listen to a range of topics. The single-level wildcard symbol is used to match one topic level, while the multi-level wildcard can match multiple levels, allowing a subscriber to, for example, receive all sensor data from a specific floor or even an entire building.

One of the defining characteristics of MQTT's architecture is its emphasis on minimalism and efficiency. The protocol uses a small packet size with fixed and variable headers that are optimized for low-bandwidth and high-latency networks. The fixed header is only two bytes for the most common message types, making it particularly suited for devices with limited memory and processing power. The variable header and payload are only included when necessary, ensuring that the protocol remains lightweight. This efficient use of network resources allows MQTT to perform reliably even over unstable or constrained connections, such as cellular networks, satellite links, or rural broadband.

The broker is not just responsible for message distribution but also plays a pivotal role in managing Quality of Service levels, session states, and retained messages. MQTT's three levels of Quality of Service give clients control over the delivery guarantees required for each message. The broker enforces these QoS agreements, ensuring that messages are delivered according to the specified reliability requirements. In the case of QoS 1 and QoS 2, the broker must store the state of each message until it is acknowledged by the subscriber, adding an additional layer of assurance in message delivery.

Another integral part of MQTT's architecture is session persistence. The broker maintains session information for clients that connect with the clean session flag set to false. This means that subscriptions and undelivered messages are stored on the broker while the client is offline and resumed once the client reconnects. This persistence is crucial in IoT environments where devices may experience temporary disconnections due to network issues or power constraints. The broker's ability to retain state simplifies the client's task, allowing devices to rejoin the network seamlessly without re-establishing all previous subscriptions or losing critical data.

The Last Will and Testament feature is another architectural component that enhances system reliability. When a client connects to the broker, it can specify a last will message along with a topic. If the client disconnects unexpectedly, the broker automatically publishes the last will message on behalf of the disconnected client. This feature is often used for device health monitoring, allowing subscribers to be notified when a device has gone offline unexpectedly, enabling quick remediation or alerts.

MQTT's architecture also supports retained messages, where publishers can send a message to a broker with a retained flag. The broker stores this message and delivers it immediately to any new subscriber of the topic, providing an efficient way to ensure that subscribers always receive the most recent state information upon subscribing, even if they were not connected when the original message was sent. This reduces the need for redundant status messages and simplifies client logic, particularly in scenarios where devices need to act on the current state as soon as they come online.

In addition to these features, MQTT's architecture accommodates a wide range of network topologies and deployment strategies. While the most common configuration involves a centralized broker deployed on a server or in the cloud, it is also possible to implement broker clustering for high availability and load balancing. Brokers can be bridged together to form interconnected networks, allowing messages to flow between geographically distributed systems while maintaining local responsiveness. This flexibility supports both small-scale, localized IoT networks and vast, global infrastructures.

Finally, MQTT's simplicity and modularity have made it compatible with modern computing paradigms such as edge computing, fog computing, and hybrid cloud-edge architectures. The broker can reside on an edge gateway, filtering and processing data locally before forwarding only relevant information to cloud services. This reduces network traffic, lowers latency, and enables real-time decision-making closer to the data source.

The MQTT architecture, while simple on the surface, is robust enough to handle the complex demands of modern IoT applications. Its focus on decoupling, efficient resource usage, and flexible message distribution has positioned it as a foundational element in building scalable, responsive, and reliable IoT ecosystems across industries. As IoT adoption continues to surge, understanding the inner workings of MQTT's architecture is essential for creating systems that are both effective and resilient.

The Publisher-Subscriber Model Explained

At the core of MQTT's functionality lies the publisher-subscriber model, a communication paradigm that offers flexibility, scalability, and efficiency, especially in distributed and resource-constrained environments like the Internet of Things. Unlike the traditional client-server model, where one system directly requests information from another, the publisher-subscriber model introduces an intermediary—the broker—that manages all interactions between devices. This model fundamentally changes how devices communicate by decoupling the sender of the message (the publisher) from the receiver of the message (the subscriber). The result is a loosely coupled system where components are independent of one another, creating a robust and adaptable communication network.

In this model, publishers are the devices or applications responsible for generating data and sending messages. These messages could be temperature readings from a weather sensor, location data from a GPS tracker, or status updates from a smart appliance. Publishers do not need to know who or what will receive their messages. They only need to send their data to the broker under a specific topic. A topic in MQTT acts as a category or label under which a message is published, helping the broker determine which subscribers are interested in receiving the data. This design eliminates the need for publishers to establish direct connections or maintain a list of recipients, greatly simplifying device logic and reducing overhead.

Subscribers, on the other hand, are devices or applications that express interest in specific topics by subscribing to them through the broker. Once subscribed, they receive all messages published to those topics in real time. A single device can subscribe to one or multiple topics depending on the information it requires. For example, a smart thermostat might subscribe to topics such as home/livingroom/temperature and home/livingroom/humidity to gather environmental data necessary for regulating the heating or cooling system. Similar to publishers, subscribers remain unaware of the identity or even the existence of the publishers. Their only point of interaction is with the broker, which delivers the data based on matching subscriptions.

The broker plays a pivotal role in the publisher-subscriber model, functioning as the central node that receives all messages from publishers and distributes them to the appropriate subscribers. When a publisher sends a message to the broker, the broker checks its internal subscription list to identify which clients are interested in the topic. It then forwards the message to all relevant subscribers. The broker is responsible for maintaining topic hierarchies, managing client sessions, handling Quality of Service levels, and ensuring efficient and reliable message delivery. This approach centralizes message routing, greatly reducing the complexity of client devices and ensuring that system scalability is managed at the broker level.

One of the primary advantages of this model is the loose coupling between publishers and subscribers. In a tightly coupled system, devices often need to maintain awareness of other devices they communicate with, meaning any change—such as adding or removing a device—could require code modifications and reconfiguration. In contrast, the publisher-subscriber model allows devices to join or leave the network dynamically without impacting other devices. This flexibility is critical in IoT applications where networks may be highly dynamic, with devices frequently going offline and online due to power constraints, environmental factors, or mobility.

Another significant benefit is the support for asynchronous communication. Because publishers and subscribers do not directly interact, they do not need to be online or available at the same time. Publishers can send data without waiting for subscribers to be available, and subscribers can receive messages when they reconnect, provided that session persistence and Quality of Service settings are configured to allow for message queuing or delivery upon reconnection. This asynchronous nature makes the model highly resilient in environments where intermittent connectivity is common.

The topic-based nature of the publisher-subscriber model allows for highly organized and efficient message filtering. Topics can be structured hierarchically to reflect logical groupings or physical arrangements within an IoT deployment. For example, a smart building might organize topics by building/floor/room/device-type, such as building1/floor2/room5/temperature or building1/floor2/room5/motion. Subscribers can also utilize wildcards to broaden their scope. A single-level wildcard matches a specific level of the hierarchy, while a multi-level wildcard can match multiple nested levels, allowing subscribers to, for instance, monitor all sensors within an entire building or focus on a specific type of sensor across different floors.

The publisher-subscriber model also simplifies the implementation of multi-recipient and broadcast communication patterns. A publisher does not need to establish multiple connections or send the same message several times to reach multiple recipients. It simply publishes once to the broker, which then handles distribution to all interested subscribers. This is particularly efficient in scenarios where the same data must be sent to numerous devices, such as broadcasting weather alerts to smart signage across a city or pushing firmware updates to a fleet of connected vehicles.

Another important aspect of the model is its inherent support for scalability. As IoT systems grow from a handful of devices to thousands or even millions of endpoints, the broker efficiently handles the increased load without overburdening the publishers or subscribers. Publishers continue sending data as usual, and subscribers continue receiving data relevant to their subscriptions, all while the broker dynamically manages the flow of information across the network. The broker can be scaled horizontally, with clustering and load-balancing mechanisms ensuring that the system remains responsive and efficient even as traffic and device counts surge.

The publisher-subscriber model is also well-suited for modern computing paradigms such as edge computing and hybrid cloud-edge systems. In these architectures, edge devices or local gateways can act as brokers, handling local publish-subscribe communication between devices and reducing the amount of data that needs to be transmitted to the cloud. This approach lowers latency, improves responsiveness, and reduces bandwidth usage, all of which are critical factors in mission-critical IoT deployments like autonomous vehicles or smart manufacturing environments.

Finally, the publisher-subscriber model provides a natural framework for event-driven architectures, where actions are triggered by specific events rather than continuous polling or direct client requests. This is particularly valuable in IoT systems, where devices need to react to environmental changes, sensor thresholds, or remote commands. For example, a smart irrigation system might subscribe to soil moisture data and trigger watering cycles only when the moisture level drops below a certain threshold. This event-driven design is efficient, reducing unnecessary device activity and conserving energy.

The publisher-subscriber model is foundational to MQTT's effectiveness in IoT ecosystems. Its decoupling of message producers and consumers, support for hierarchical topic filtering, and centralization of message routing through the broker provide a robust, scalable, and efficient communication pattern. Whether used in small-scale smart home setups or massive industrial systems, this model offers the adaptability and simplicity required to meet the diverse challenges of the IoT landscape.

MQTT Brokers: The Heart of the System

The MQTT broker is the central component that enables the entire publish-subscribe mechanism to function effectively. Without the broker, there would be no coordination between publishers and subscribers, no reliable message routing, and no session management. The broker is, quite literally, the heart of any MQTT-based communication system, responsible for receiving, filtering, and delivering messages to clients based on the topics to which they subscribe. Its role is to ensure that the right data reaches the right devices at the right time, even in complex, distributed, or resource-constrained environments.

The primary responsibility of the MQTT broker is message routing. When a publisher sends a message to the broker, it is accompanied by a topic, which acts as a label or category for the message. The broker checks its list of active client subscriptions and identifies which clients have expressed interest in that particular topic. Once the broker has matched the topic to the corresponding subscribers, it forwards the message to all of them. This eliminates the need for publishers to have knowledge of the subscribers or to manage multiple direct communication channels. The broker becomes the central hub through which all messages flow, reducing complexity on the device side and streamlining the entire network.

Beyond routing, the broker also manages topic hierarchies and supports wildcard subscriptions. This allows for powerful filtering mechanisms that help scale systems with hundreds or thousands of topics. For example, a broker might be managing a smart city network where devices publish data under topics such as city1/traffic/sensor1 or city1/airquality/sensor3. Subscribers can specify subscriptions using wildcards, such as city1/traffic/#, to capture all traffic-related messages under a certain branch. The broker is responsible for interpreting these wildcards and efficiently matching them to the correct topics, ensuring subscribers receive all relevant data without being overloaded with unrelated information.

Another critical function of the broker is the enforcement of Quality of Service (QoS) levels. MQTT provides three QoS levels to balance message delivery assurance against network overhead. At QoS 0, messages are delivered at most once with no acknowledgment. At QoS 1, messages are guaranteed to be delivered at least once, with acknowledgments sent by the subscriber. At QoS 2, messages are assured to be delivered exactly once using a two-phase acknowledgment process. The broker handles all these mechanisms, tracking message IDs, maintaining state, and ensuring that messages meet their QoS agreements before being forwarded to subscribers. This is particularly important in scenarios where the reliability of data delivery is paramount, such as in industrial automation or healthcare monitoring.

Session management is another area where the broker plays a vital role. When clients connect to the broker, they can choose to establish either a clean session or a persistent session. In a clean session, all subscriptions and session state information are discarded when the client disconnects. In contrast, a persistent session stores this information on the broker, allowing clients to resume where they left off upon reconnection. The broker retains undelivered messages for clients with persistent sessions, ensuring that no critical data is lost due to temporary disconnections. This is crucial for IoT deployments where devices frequently operate on intermittent connections or constrained power supplies, such as battery-operated sensors in remote locations.

The broker is also responsible for implementing the Last Will and Testament (LWT) mechanism. When a client connects, it can provide a last will message along with a designated topic. If the client disconnects unexpectedly, the broker will automatically publish this last will message on behalf of the client. This feature helps in fault detection and network health monitoring. For instance, in a fleet management application, a disconnected vehicle telematics unit might trigger an automatic alert through the broker, notifying the operations center that the device is offline and immediate attention may be required.

Security and access control are other important broker functions. While the MQTT protocol itself is lightweight and does not mandate specific security mechanisms, the broker is typically configured to enforce authentication and authorization policies. Clients may be required to present valid credentials, such as usernames and passwords or client certificates, before being allowed to connect. The broker can also implement fine-grained access controls, restricting which topics a client is allowed to publish to or subscribe from. Combined with Transport Layer Security (TLS) for encryption, the broker ensures that sensitive data transmitted across the MQTT network is protected from unauthorized access and eavesdropping.

The scalability of MQTT systems is largely dependent on the broker's capabilities. A single broker can efficiently handle thousands of simultaneous client connections, but as IoT systems grow, brokers may need to be clustered to distribute the load and provide high availability. Broker clustering allows multiple broker instances to share the responsibility of message routing and session management, ensuring that the system remains responsive under heavy traffic and is resilient to node failures. In geographically distributed networks, brokers can be bridged together, allowing messages to be relayed across different regions while maintaining local responsiveness. This is particularly useful in large-scale IoT applications like smart grids or global logistics networks.

Modern MQTT brokers often include extensive monitoring and diagnostic tools that provide real-time visibility into system health and performance. Operators can view metrics such as the number of connected clients, message throughput, latency, dropped messages, and system resource usage. These insights are critical for troubleshooting, capacity planning, and optimizing system performance. Advanced brokers may also offer logging and auditing features to track message flows, security events, and client activity over time, which is essential for compliance with regulatory requirements and forensics.

The broker's role extends even further in hybrid cloud-edge architectures. In edge computing scenarios, brokers may be deployed on local gateways to facilitate low-latency communication between edge devices while selectively forwarding data to cloud-based brokers for aggregation, analysis, and long-term storage. This architecture optimizes bandwidth usage, reduces latency, and ensures that critical decisions can be made closer to where the data originates. The broker thus acts as a bridge between local, time-sensitive processing and centralized, large-scale data analytics.

In essence, the MQTT broker is the orchestrator of the entire messaging system. It simplifies the logic required on client devices by centralizing the complexity of message routing, session management, QoS enforcement, and security. Whether deployed in small home automation networks or vast industrial IoT ecosystems, the broker ensures that communication between devices is efficient, reliable, and secure. As IoT networks continue to expand, the MQTT broker remains a pivotal element in building resilient and scalable communication infrastructures that connect devices across the world.

MQTT Clients and Devices

In the MQTT ecosystem, clients are the active participants that interact with the broker to send and receive messages. These clients can be physical devices, such as sensors, actuators, gateways, and embedded systems, or they can be software applications running on servers, desktops, or cloud infrastructure. Regardless of their form, MQTT clients serve as the interface between the physical or digital world and the messaging system, enabling data to flow throughout the network. Each client is capable of assuming one or both roles within the MQTT protocol: that of a publisher, which sends messages to the broker, or a subscriber, which receives messages from the broker. In many practical deployments, a single device may act as both, depending on its functionality and purpose within the system.

MQTT clients are designed to operate in highly diverse environments, from simple microcontrollers embedded in remote sensor nodes to powerful backend services running in cloud data centers. This flexibility is one of the reasons MQTT has become so prevalent across IoT use cases. A client could be a low-power temperature sensor installed on a farm, a wearable health monitoring device transmitting patient vitals, or a smart streetlight controller that both publishes its operational status and subscribes to control commands from a central system. The protocol's lightweight design allows it to run efficiently even on devices with limited processing power, memory, and network bandwidth, which is critical in IoT scenarios where resource constraints are common.

When an MQTT client initiates communication with the broker, it must first establish a connection. This connection is typically established over TCP/IP, although MQTT can also be used over WebSockets in certain applications. Once connected, the client maintains an open session with the broker, allowing it to publish messages, subscribe to topics, or perform both actions simultaneously. The connection remains active until the client explicitly disconnects or until the broker detects a timeout or an unexpected termination. MQTT's keep-alive mechanism ensures that the broker and client maintain awareness of each other's availability, sending periodic pings to confirm that the connection remains active.

Once connected, clients use the publish-subscribe mechanism to exchange data with other parts of the system. A publisher client creates a message payload, which could be any form of data such as a numerical value, JSON object, or binary file, and sends it to the broker along with the topic that categorizes the message. On the receiving end, subscriber clients express interest in one or more topics by registering those subscriptions with the broker. The broker then automatically routes incoming messages to all subscribed clients, enabling asynchronous, decoupled communication between devices.

MQTT clients also leverage the protocol's Quality of Service (QoS) levels to define how messages should be delivered. This gives developers control over the balance between reliability and resource consumption. A client might publish non-critical environmental data at QoS 0 to conserve bandwidth and processing power, while mission-critical control commands could be sent at QoS 2 to ensure that they are delivered exactly once. Clients are responsible for specifying the QoS level when publishing or subscribing, and the broker enforces the required delivery guarantees based on these settings. This allows a single system to support a variety of communication needs, ranging from lightweight sensor data to highly reliable command and control messages.

Devices acting as MQTT clients are often deployed in diverse and sometimes harsh environments, such as industrial facilities, agricultural fields, transportation fleets, or smart cities. Many of these devices must be able to operate with intermittent or unreliable network connectivity. MQTT clients are designed to handle such conditions gracefully by incorporating session persistence and automatic reconnect logic. When a client connects to the broker, it can specify whether it wants to create a clean session or maintain a persistent one. In a persistent session, the broker retains the client's subscriptions and queued messages while the client is offline, resuming delivery once the client reconnects. This is essential for IoT devices that may experience power-saving sleep modes, mobile network coverage gaps, or power outages.

Security is also an important consideration for MQTT clients. While the MQTT protocol itself is agnostic to specific security mechanisms, clients are typically configured to authenticate themselves with the broker using credentials such as a username and password or X.509 certificates. Transport Layer Security (TLS) is commonly used to encrypt data exchanged between clients and brokers, protecting against eavesdropping and tampering. Additionally, some brokers enforce fine-grained access control policies, allowing clients to only publish to or subscribe from authorized topics. Clients, therefore, need to be provisioned with the appropriate security credentials and configurations to ensure compliance with system-wide security requirements.

MQTT clients are highly versatile in terms of how they are implemented. Developers can choose from a wide range of MQTT client libraries available in most programming languages, including Python, C, C++, Java, JavaScript, Go, and Rust. This allows MQTT clients to be built into various types of devices and applications. For instance, embedded developers may use lightweight C libraries to integrate MQTT into constrained microcontrollers, while cloud architects might leverage Python or Java libraries to develop scalable backend services that aggregate and process data from thousands of edge devices.

Beyond embedded and backend systems, MQTT clients also play a crucial role in bridging IoT devices with user interfaces and data visualization tools. Mobile applications, web dashboards, and desktop software can act as MQTT clients, subscribing to topics and displaying real-time data streams to users. For example, a mobile app might receive alerts from a smart home security system, while a web-based dashboard provides operators with live telemetry from industrial equipment. This seamless flow of information from device to user is a key enabler of actionable insights and remote control within IoT ecosystems.

Some MQTT clients also serve as protocol translators or gateways, bridging MQTT networks with other communication protocols such as HTTP, Modbus, BACnet, or proprietary industrial protocols. In this role, an MQTT client may receive data from non-MQTT devices, repackage it into MQTT messages, and forward it to the broker. This enables legacy systems or devices that do not natively support MQTT to integrate into modern IoT infrastructures.

Overall, MQTT clients are the building blocks that bring the protocol to life in the field. Whether embedded inside a single-board computer monitoring soil moisture, part of a smart meter reporting energy usage, or running within a cloud platform to aggregate sensor data for big data analysis, these clients are essential to the operation of MQTT-based communication networks. Their ability to operate in a wide range of environments, communicate asynchronously, and leverage robust QoS and security features makes them indispensable components of modern IoT solutions. Through MQTT clients, the physical and digital worlds become interconnected, enabling automation, optimization, and intelligence across industries.

Connecting to an MQTT Broker

Establishing a connection between an MQTT client and an MQTT broker is the first critical step in enabling message exchange within an

MQTT-based communication system. This connection process may seem simple on the surface, but it involves several important stages that ensure the client can reliably communicate with the broker, authenticate if necessary, and begin publishing or subscribing to topics. Whether the MQTT client is a low-power sensor node, a powerful cloud application, or a mobile device, this connection process must be robust, secure, and efficient to meet the demands of modern IoT environments.

The MQTT client initiates the connection by establishing a TCP/IP session with the broker. MQTT typically runs over the Transmission Control Protocol because TCP provides reliable, ordered, and error-checked delivery of packets between the client and broker. In many cases, this connection is made over port 1883, the default for unencrypted MQTT traffic, or port 8883 when encrypted communication using TLS (Transport Layer Security) is required. Some applications use MQTT over WebSockets, particularly when connecting browsers or web applications to MQTT brokers, as WebSockets enable bi-directional communication over standard HTTP ports such as 80 or 443.

Once the TCP connection is established, the MQTT client sends a CONNECT control packet to the broker. This packet contains several key elements that inform the broker about the client's identity, configuration, and connection preferences. The client ID is one of the most important fields in the CONNECT packet. This identifier must be unique for each client connected to the broker, as it is used to track sessions, manage persistent subscriptions, and prevent session collisions. Depending on the implementation, the client ID might be generated dynamically, derived from the device's MAC address or serial number, or assigned statically by the system integrator.

The CONNECT packet may also include optional fields for authentication. If the broker requires client authentication, the client must provide a username and password as part of the connection request. Some systems implement more advanced authentication methods, such as TLS client certificates, OAuth tokens, or custom authentication plugins configured on the broker side. The broker verifies the client's credentials during the connection process, allowing or denying access based on predefined security policies. This authentication step is critical in IoT environments where unauthorized access to the messaging system could compromise sensitive data or control critical infrastructure.

Another important component of the CONNECT packet is the clean session flag. This flag indicates whether the client wishes to establish a new session each time it connects or to resume a previous session. If the clean session flag is set to true, the broker will discard any previously stored session state, such as undelivered messages and topic subscriptions. This is often used by clients that only require transient communication or publish occasional status updates. If the clean session flag is set to false, the broker will retain the session's state information, allowing the client to resume its previous subscriptions and receive any messages that were published while it was offline. Persistent sessions are especially valuable in IoT scenarios where devices frequently disconnect due to power-saving modes or intermittent network conditions.

As part of the connection process, clients may also define a keep-alive interval. The keep-alive interval, measured in seconds, specifies how often the client must communicate with the broker to signal that it is still active. If no communication occurs within the specified interval, the broker assumes the client is no longer reachable and will close the connection. To comply with the keep-alive policy, clients typically send PINGREQ packets to the broker at regular intervals. The broker responds with a PINGRESP packet, confirming the connection remains alive. This mechanism helps maintain network stability and ensures that disconnected clients are detected promptly.

A unique feature of MQTT's connection process is the Last Will and Testament (LWT) mechanism. When connecting, a client can specify a will message along with a topic. If the client unexpectedly disconnects without sending a DISCONNECT packet, the broker publishes the LWT message on the specified topic, notifying subscribers that the client is offline. This is a vital feature in systems where monitoring device availability is critical. For instance, in an industrial monitoring setup, a machinery sensor might provide an LWT that alerts supervisors if the sensor goes offline unexpectedly, enabling quick intervention.

After sending the CONNECT packet, the client waits for a CONNACK packet from the broker. This packet indicates whether the connection has been accepted or rejected and provides a return code explaining the broker's response. A successful connection is followed by the client entering an active session state where it can begin publishing messages, subscribing to topics, or both. If the broker rejects the connection, the client must handle the error, which might be due to invalid credentials, incorrect client ID, or broker configuration settings such as connection throttling or IP restrictions.

Once connected, the client can dynamically subscribe to topics using the SUBSCRIBE packet, specifying the desired topic filters and Quality of Service levels. This enables the client to start receiving real-time updates on topics of interest. The client can also begin publishing data to the broker using PUBLISH packets, which contain the topic, message payload, and additional flags related to QoS, retained messages, or duplicate delivery indicators. The broker manages message routing and ensures that published messages are delivered to all clients subscribed to the corresponding topics.

The connection process does not end with a simple handshake; it is continuously monitored and managed throughout the session. MQTT clients must be designed to handle scenarios such as unexpected disconnections, broker reboots, or network outages. Many MQTT client libraries include automatic reconnect features, allowing the client to retry the connection process when communication with the broker is lost. This automatic reconnect logic ensures that devices in remote or harsh environments can maintain reliable communication with minimal intervention, even in the face of network instability.

For developers and system architects, understanding the connection flow between clients and brokers is essential to designing resilient and secure IoT systems. Factors such as session persistence, security credentials, keep-alive settings, and LWT configuration must be carefully planned to align with the operational requirements of the deployment. Whether building a smart home system, a fleet management platform, or a real-time industrial control network, establishing reliable connections between MQTT clients and brokers is the first step toward enabling scalable, event-driven communication across distributed devices and applications.

Topics and Topic Hierarchies

Topics are a fundamental element of MQTT, providing the structure through which messages are organized, categorized, and routed between publishers and subscribers. Every message sent through an MQTT broker is associated with a specific topic, which acts as the communication channel for that message. Topics are not static entities or pre-registered channels. Instead, they are dynamic, meaning publishers and subscribers can define and use topics on the fly without prior configuration in the broker. This level of flexibility is one of the reasons MQTT is so effective at supporting diverse and dynamic IoT ecosystems.

A topic in MQTT is a UTF-8 string that defines a logical path or namespace to which messages are published and from which subscribers receive data. Topics are structured hierarchically using forward slashes as delimiters. This hierarchy resembles a file directory system, where each level provides an additional layer of categorization and granularity. For example, a topic might be structured as smartbuilding/floor1/room5/temperature. In this case, smartbuilding is the root level, followed by floor1, then room5, and finally the specific data type, temperature. This hierarchical approach allows for organized and scalable systems where devices and services can easily identify the source and context of the data.

The use of hierarchical topics is especially valuable in large-scale IoT deployments where multiple devices, sensors, or services need to operate within the same network. In a smart city scenario, for instance, a topic hierarchy might reflect the structure of different districts, streets, or buildings. A streetlight sensor in district1/streetA/lamp5 might publish its operational status or energy consumption to that specific topic, allowing only the relevant subscribers, such as the city's maintenance system or energy management platform, to receive and process that data. The hierarchical model ensures that data remains well-organized, even as the number of devices and messages grows exponentially.

Subscribers in MQTT have the capability to subscribe to one or multiple topics and, more importantly, to leverage wildcard characters to broaden their scope of interest. There are two types of wildcards in MQTT: the single-level wildcard and the multi-level wildcard. The single-level wildcard is represented by the plus symbol and matches exactly one hierarchical level within the topic structure. For example, a subscription to smartbuilding/+/room5/temperature would match smartbuilding/floor1/room5/temperature and smartbuilding/floor2/room5/temperature, regardless of which floor the room is on. This allows a subscriber to monitor the temperature of room5 across all floors without needing to subscribe to each floor individually.

The multi-level wildcard, represented by the hash symbol, matches all remaining hierarchical levels starting from a specific point in the topic. A subscription to smartbuilding/# would match all topics starting with smartbuilding, including smartbuilding/floor1/room1/humidity, smartbuilding/floor3/room6/light, and any other nested topics under the smartbuilding root. This wildcard is particularly useful for services that need to aggregate or monitor large swaths of data from an entire system. For example, an operations dashboard might use a multi-level wildcard to receive all sensor data from an entire smart building or campus.

Topic design is a crucial consideration when architecting MQTT-based systems. The clarity and logic of topic hierarchies directly impact the efficiency and maintainability of the communication system. A well-structured topic hierarchy not only makes it easier for developers to design applications but also improves system performance by reducing unnecessary message traffic. For instance, if topics are too broad and flat, subscribers may end up receiving more messages than they need, forcing them to filter out irrelevant data locally. Conversely, overly granular or deeply nested topics might create excessive fragmentation, making it harder for subscribers to retrieve data efficiently.

In addition to routing messages, MQTT topics play a role in retained messages. When a publisher sends a message with the retained flag set to true, the broker stores the message on the corresponding topic and automatically delivers it to any new subscribers of that topic. This is particularly useful for state information or system status updates. For example, a smart thermostat might publish its current operating mode—such as heating or cooling—to a retained topic like home/livingroom/thermostat/mode. Any client that subsequently subscribes to this topic will immediately receive the latest retained message, ensuring it has up-to-date information without waiting for the next update from the device.

The broker does not interpret the meaning of topic strings; it only performs simple string matching and wildcard resolution based on client subscriptions. This design decision keeps MQTT brokers lightweight and efficient while leaving the responsibility for topic organization and naming conventions to developers and system architects. To avoid confusion and ensure scalability, teams often establish naming standards or conventions that are consistent across their entire deployment. Common conventions might include using lowercase letters, separating words with underscores, and consistently ordering hierarchical levels from general to specific.

It is important to note that MQTT topics are case-sensitive. A topic like smartbuilding/floor1/room5/temperature is distinct from SmartBuilding/floor1/room5/temperature. Inconsistent use of casing can lead to unexpected behavior, such as missed messages or duplicate subscriptions. Likewise, topic strings cannot contain wildcard symbols in their published form; wildcards are reserved exclusively for subscription patterns and are not valid in topics used by publishers.

While MQTT topics are highly flexible, they also contribute to system security when combined with broker-level access control mechanisms. Many brokers support access control lists (ACLs) that define which topics a given client is allowed to publish to or subscribe from. This helps enforce security boundaries within the topic hierarchy, ensuring that devices or services only have access to data they are authorized to use. For example, a temperature sensor in room5 might be restricted to publishing only under topics within the smartbuilding/floor1/room5 branch, preventing it from inadvertently or maliciously sending data to unrelated parts of the system.

The structure of topics also facilitates the implementation of multi-tenant systems, where different clients or customer environments are logically separated within the same broker instance. A cloud-based IoT platform might assign each customer a unique namespace, such as customerA/# and customerB/#, ensuring that each tenant's devices and services operate within isolated topic trees.

At the core of MQTT's design philosophy is simplicity paired with flexibility, and topics embody this principle perfectly. Through hierarchical structuring and wildcard subscriptions, topics enable MQTT to support everything from simple point-to-point communication in a home automation system to complex, distributed architectures in industrial and smart city deployments. Understanding and applying best practices in topic hierarchy design is vital to unlocking the full potential of MQTT and ensuring the long-term success of any IoT implementation.

Quality of Service (QoS) Levels

The Quality of Service (QoS) levels in MQTT are one of the protocol's most defining features, enabling developers to tailor the reliability of message delivery to the specific needs of their IoT applications. In an environment where devices range from simple battery-powered sensors to sophisticated backend systems, not every message requires the same delivery guarantees. MQTT addresses this by offering three distinct QoS levels that balance reliability, network efficiency, and resource consumption. By understanding these QoS levels and applying them effectively, IoT architects can optimize their systems for both performance and dependability.

The first QoS level is QoS 0, also referred to as at most once delivery. At this level, a message is sent by the publisher to the broker and then forwarded to subscribers without any form of acknowledgment. This is a fire-and-forget approach where the message may be delivered once, or it may be lost altogether if there is a network failure, broker downtime, or client disconnection during transmission. QoS 0 is the most lightweight and efficient option, as it minimizes network overhead and avoids the need for additional control packets to confirm message delivery. It is particularly suitable for use cases where occasional message loss is acceptable or where data is sent frequently and redundancy is naturally built into the system. Examples include non-critical sensor data such as environmental temperature readings or periodic status updates where losing a single data point does not compromise the system's overall functionality.

The second QoS level is QoS 1, known as at least once delivery. This level ensures that the message is delivered to the intended recipient at least one time but could potentially result in duplicate messages if acknowledgments are lost and the message is retransmitted. In this mode, after a publisher sends a message to the broker, the broker must respond with a PUBACK acknowledgment packet to confirm receipt. If the publisher does not receive this acknowledgment within a certain timeout period, it will resend the message. Similarly, when the broker delivers the message to subscribers, the subscriber must acknowledge it, and the broker may retransmit the message if no acknowledgment is received. While this increases network traffic slightly compared to QoS 0, it provides a higher level of delivery assurance, making it a popular choice in systems where occasional duplication is manageable but data loss is unacceptable. Applications such as monitoring alarms, operational status updates for machinery, or critical event logs often rely on QoS 1 to ensure that data is reliably transmitted even in the face of network instability.

The highest level of service is QoS 2, referred to as exactly once delivery. This level guarantees that each message is delivered to its destination exactly one time, eliminating the possibility of duplicates entirely. QoS 2 achieves this by using a four-step handshake process between the publisher, broker, and subscriber. The process involves the exchange of PUBLISH, PUBREC, PUBREL, and PUBCOMP control packets to confirm receipt and processing of the message at every step of the transmission chain. While this adds additional overhead and complexity to the system, it is essential for use cases where duplicate messages could lead to erroneous behavior or data corruption. Financial transaction systems, industrial control commands, and mission-critical healthcare applications are examples where QoS 2 might be necessary to ensure that each instruction or data point is processed only once.

In practice, the choice of QoS level is not always dictated solely by the criticality of the data but also by network conditions and device capabilities. Resource-constrained devices may opt for QoS 0 to conserve battery life and bandwidth, while backend systems with reliable connections and high processing power might safely use QoS 2 where required. The broker plays a central role in enforcing QoS contracts. When a publisher sends a message at a certain QoS level, the broker must handle the message according to that level, ensuring that the delivery requirements are met for all subscribers, even if they each have different QoS requests. For example, a single message published at QoS 2 could be forwarded to one subscriber at QoS 2, another at QoS 1, and yet another at QoS 0, depending on the subscription requests of each client.

It is also important to recognize that higher QoS levels introduce trade-offs. While QoS 2 offers the highest reliability, it also increases latency and network usage due to the additional packet exchanges required. In systems where bandwidth is constrained or where ultra-low latency is a priority, developers may choose to rely on QoS 0 or QoS 1 and compensate for potential message loss through application-level logic, such as periodic retries or redundant data streams. Balancing these trade-offs is an essential part of designing efficient MQTT-based systems, and each application must be evaluated based on its tolerance for message loss, duplicates, and latency.

The interaction between QoS levels and MQTT's session persistence further enhances the reliability of the system. When clients connect with persistent sessions, the broker retains undelivered QoS 1 and QoS 2 messages for those clients even if they temporarily disconnect. Upon reconnection, the broker resumes delivery of the queued messages in accordance with their respective QoS levels. This capability is critical for mobile or battery-powered devices that frequently switch between online and offline states. In contrast, QoS 0 messages are not retained by the broker if a client is offline when the message is published, as the protocol assumes no delivery guarantee at this level.

QoS levels also play an integral role in message retention strategies. For example, when combined with retained messages, a QoS 1 or QoS 2 message can ensure that new subscribers receive a reliable last known value upon subscribing to a topic. This pattern is often used in smart home and industrial applications to deliver the current state of devices, such as the latest temperature reading from a thermostat or the operational status of a production line.

In MQTT deployments, system architects must carefully design message flows with appropriate QoS levels to meet business and technical requirements. By leveraging MQTT's flexible QoS system, developers can build highly responsive, resilient, and resource-efficient networks that perform well across a wide spectrum of applications and conditions. Whether prioritizing bandwidth efficiency, delivery assurance, or system responsiveness, QoS provides the necessary tools to adapt MQTT to virtually any IoT scenario.

Session Management and Persistence

Session management and persistence in MQTT are fundamental mechanisms that ensure the continuity and reliability of communication between clients and brokers, even in the face of intermittent connectivity, network failures, or device restarts. The MQTT protocol is designed to accommodate a wide range of devices, many of which operate in environments where stable network conditions cannot be guaranteed. Whether dealing with battery-powered IoT sensors that periodically enter sleep mode or mobile devices that traverse different network zones, session management allows MQTT clients to maintain their subscriptions and message flow integrity despite disruptions.

An MQTT session begins the moment a client connects to the broker. When establishing this connection, the client specifies its session preferences through the clean session flag within the CONNECT packet. This flag instructs the broker on how to handle session state data, including subscriptions and undelivered messages. If the clean session flag is set to true, the broker treats the connection as transient. It will not retain any information once the client disconnects, effectively starting fresh each time the client reconnects. This mode is suitable for clients that only require short-lived interactions or whose communications are not dependent on prior session history.

On the other hand, when the clean session flag is set to false, the client requests a persistent session. This means that the broker will store the client's subscription information and any messages with Quality of Service levels 1 or 2 that could not be delivered while the client was offline. When the client reconnects, the broker resumes the session and ensures that all pending messages are delivered in accordance with their respective QoS levels. This persistent session model is indispensable in IoT environments where devices may frequently lose connectivity due to power-saving cycles, unreliable network coverage, or environmental factors beyond the device's control.

The broker plays a central role in managing session data. For clients with persistent sessions, it stores subscriptions, undelivered QoS 1 and QoS 2 messages, and certain flags that indicate session status. This persistence allows devices to avoid re-subscribing to topics each time they reconnect, reducing overhead and simplifying client logic. Instead, devices can resume their session and immediately begin receiving messages as if they had remained continuously online. This capability is particularly useful in large-scale IoT deployments, such as agricultural monitoring systems, where remote devices may rely on intermittent cellular connections or satellite links and need to conserve battery life by disconnecting between data transmissions.

The session state also affects how messages are handled when a client unexpectedly disconnects. If a device publishing critical telemetry data suddenly loses its connection, any retained messages in a persistent session will still be available for subscribers who reconnect later. For subscriber clients, any QoS 1 or QoS 2 messages published during their offline period will be stored by the broker and delivered once the client comes back online. This ensures data continuity even in unstable environments where network conditions may fluctuate.

The session management system in MQTT also interacts with the protocol's Last Will and Testament (LWT) feature. When a client establishes a connection and provides an LWT message, the broker retains this message as part of the session state. If the broker detects an abnormal disconnection from the client, such as a sudden loss of connection without a proper DISCONNECT packet, it will publish the LWT message to the specified topic on behalf of the disconnected client. This mechanism provides other clients with immediate notification of device failure or unavailability, supporting system-wide reliability and fault tolerance.

Another key aspect of session management is how MQTT brokers manage retained messages independently from persistent sessions. Retained messages are stored at the topic level by the broker, regardless of individual client sessions. When a new client subscribes to a topic with a retained message, the broker immediately sends the retained message to the subscriber, ensuring that it has the latest status or data point available. This feature is frequently used to convey system states, such as the current on/off status of a smart appliance, the latest temperature reading from a sensor, or the operational mode of industrial equipment.

Session persistence is also vital in supporting MQTT's Quality of Service guarantees. For QoS 1 and QoS 2 messages, the broker must retain message delivery state information during disconnections to comply with the promised delivery semantics. This includes tracking message identifiers, acknowledgment statuses, and retransmission requirements. Without session persistence, devices would risk losing messages during periods of disconnection, leading to gaps in data continuity or missed events.

MQTT session management contributes significantly to reducing network and device resource consumption. Devices that rely on persistent sessions avoid the overhead of repeatedly sending subscription requests, which is particularly beneficial in networks where bandwidth is limited or where devices must conserve power. Instead of continuously polling or re-establishing their place in the system, clients can rely on the broker's stored session state to seamlessly resume operations with minimal packet exchanges.

In addition to client-broker interactions, session persistence plays a role in scalability and system design. In environments with thousands of connected devices, efficient session management reduces broker load by minimizing repetitive subscription traffic and streamlining message handling. The broker's ability to offload session state to persistent storage or distributed clusters further enhances system resilience, ensuring that session data is protected against broker failures or restarts.

Different MQTT broker implementations offer varying levels of customization and control over session persistence. Some brokers allow administrators to configure session expiry intervals, specifying how long session data should be retained after a client disconnects. For example, a session might expire after one hour, one day, or indefinitely, depending on the system's operational requirements. This adds another layer of flexibility, enabling system architects to balance persistence, resource usage, and system behavior.

Ultimately, session management and persistence are critical for enabling the reliability and efficiency that IoT applications demand. Whether ensuring the uninterrupted delivery of telemetry data from remote sensors, maintaining seamless user experiences in smart home ecosystems, or enabling real-time command and control in industrial automation systems, these MQTT features provide the infrastructure needed for resilient communication. By leveraging persistent sessions appropriately, developers and architects can build systems that gracefully handle the unpredictability of real-world networks and deliver dependable performance across a broad range of IoT use cases.

MQTT Control Packets Deep Dive

The MQTT protocol operates through a series of defined control packets that manage every stage of communication between clients and brokers. Each control packet serves a specific purpose within the protocol, and understanding how they function is essential to mastering MQTT's operation. These packets are the building blocks of MQTT sessions, message exchanges, subscription handling, and session termination. Despite the protocol's lightweight design, the control packet system is robust enough to handle a wide range of communication requirements, from simple telemetry transmissions to highly reliable transactional messaging in critical IoT systems.

The lifecycle of an MQTT session begins with the CONNECT packet. This packet is sent by the client to the broker to initiate a connection and establish the session's parameters. The CONNECT packet contains essential information such as the client ID, username and password (if authentication is required), the clean session flag, the keep-alive interval, and optionally the Last Will and Testament configuration. This packet signals the broker that a client is requesting to start a new session or resume a previous persistent session. The broker responds with a CONNACK packet, which confirms whether the connection has been accepted or rejected. The CONNACK packet contains a return code that indicates the result, including successful connection or specific error conditions like identifier rejection, authentication failure, or broker unavailability.

Once a session is established, the client may send SUBSCRIBE packets to inform the broker of the topics it wishes to receive messages from. A SUBSCRIBE packet contains one or more topic filters and specifies the desired Quality of Service level for each subscription. This packet allows the client to dynamically select which data streams it is interested in during the course of the session. After processing the subscription request, the broker responds with a SUBACK packet that acknowledges receipt of the subscription and confirms the QoS level granted for each topic. This acknowledgment is crucial because brokers might not always honor the client's requested QoS and may downgrade it depending on system policies.

Publishing data is handled through the PUBLISH packet, one of the most commonly used control packets in MQTT. A PUBLISH packet contains the topic under which the message will be categorized, the actual payload of the message, and additional flags that control how the broker should handle the message. These flags include settings such as the retained message flag, which instructs the broker to store the message for future subscribers, and the duplicate delivery flag, which is relevant for retransmissions under certain QoS levels. The PUBLISH packet also includes a QoS level that determines the delivery guarantees associated with the message. Depending on the QoS level, the PUBLISH packet may trigger additional control packets to manage acknowledgments and retransmissions.

For QoS 1, the broker responds to a PUBLISH packet with a PUBACK packet to acknowledge successful receipt of the message. If the PUBACK is not received by the client within a set time frame, the client will resend the PUBLISH packet with the duplicate flag set. This mechanism ensures that the message is delivered at least once. For QoS 2, which guarantees exactly once delivery, the process is more elaborate and involves a four-step handshake. After receiving a QoS 2 PUBLISH packet, the broker responds with a PUBREC packet to indicate that it has received the message and will not process duplicates. The client then sends a PUBREL packet, signaling that it considers the message transaction complete. Finally, the broker responds with a PUBCOMP packet, confirming that the message has been fully processed and no further action is required. This multi-stage exchange ensures that both the publisher and broker agree on the successful delivery of the message without duplication.

In addition to publishing and subscribing, clients can remove existing subscriptions using the UNSUBSCRIBE packet. This packet allows the client to specify one or more topics it no longer wishes to receive messages from. The broker responds to this packet with an UNSUBACK packet, acknowledging that the subscription has been removed. This feature is particularly useful in dynamic IoT applications where devices may need to modify their subscriptions based on changing operational conditions or priorities. For instance, a mobile sensor might subscribe to different regional topics depending on its current location and later unsubscribe when it moves out of a coverage zone.

Maintaining an active MQTT session also involves periodic keep-alive signaling, managed by the PINGREQ and PINGRESP control packets. The client sends a PINGREQ packet to the broker when it has not sent any other packets during the configured keep-alive interval. The broker responds with a PINGRESP packet to confirm that the connection is still active. This lightweight heartbeat mechanism helps both the client and broker detect broken or idle connections without relying on application-level pings or additional networking overhead.

The MQTT session is terminated with the DISCONNECT packet. When a client intends to close the session cleanly, it sends a DISCONNECT packet to the broker, signaling that it no longer wishes to communicate. This allows the broker to release any session-related resources, such as subscriptions or pending QoS 1 and QoS 2 messages, depending on whether the session was persistent or clean. The DISCONNECT packet also prevents the broker from publishing the client's Last Will and Testament, as the orderly disconnection indicates that the client is shutting down intentionally.

Each control packet in MQTT has a fixed header, which is mandatory, and in many cases, an optional variable header and payload. The fixed header includes the packet type and flags specific to that type, while the variable header and payload carry additional information as needed. This design allows MQTT to minimize overhead by including only the data necessary for each specific operation. For example, a simple QoS o PUBLISH packet for telemetry data may contain only a few bytes beyond the fixed header, making it exceptionally efficient for constrained devices and bandwidth-limited environments.

Understanding MQTT control packets at this granular level is key to designing systems that are both efficient and reliable. Developers can fine-tune their applications by knowing exactly how each packet type interacts with brokers and clients, ensuring that the messaging flow operates smoothly across a wide range of IoT deployments. From initiating secure and persistent sessions to ensuring reliable message delivery and managing resource-efficient keep-alive mechanisms, MQTT's control packet structure provides the essential framework that underpins the protocol's reputation for lightweight, scalable communication. Each packet plays a precise role in coordinating client-broker interactions, supporting the robustness and flexibility required by modern IoT systems.

The Role of Keep-Alive and Last Will

Within the MQTT protocol, two essential mechanisms contribute significantly to maintaining system reliability and network stability: the keep-alive mechanism and the Last Will and Testament feature. Both elements serve different purposes but work together to ensure the continuity and resilience of the communication between clients and the broker, even in adverse conditions. These features are particularly crucial in IoT ecosystems where devices are deployed in remote, mobile, or unreliable network environments, where unexpected disconnections and power losses are common.

The keep-alive mechanism is a heartbeat system that helps maintain the connection between the client and the broker. It is a time-based feature where the client informs the broker of the maximum amount of time that should pass without any data exchange. This value is specified in seconds and is sent to the broker when the client initiates the session using the CONNECT control packet. The broker expects to receive some form of communication from the client within this interval, either a normal MQTT control packet such as PUBLISH, SUBSCRIBE, or UNSUBSCRIBE, or a special PINGREQ packet specifically meant to maintain the session. If the broker does not receive any packets from the client within one and a half times the keep-alive interval, it considers the client to be unavailable and closes the connection.

This mechanism is especially important for detecting silent failures or abnormal disconnections, which can occur when a device loses power unexpectedly or experiences network disruptions. Without a keep-alive feature, the broker would have no way of knowing that a client is no longer reachable, leading to stale sessions and potential resource wastage. By using the keep-alive interval effectively, the broker can quickly and efficiently free up system resources, such as retained session data and QoS message queues, for other active clients. It also plays a role in preventing the accumulation of ghost clients, which could degrade system performance or cause miscommunication in large-scale deployments.

For the client, sending PINGREQ packets at regular intervals when idle ensures that it remains connected even during periods of inactivity. This is particularly useful for devices that may only publish or subscribe to data infrequently but still need to maintain a persistent session for when data transmission becomes necessary. Devices operating on low-power or mobile networks benefit from being able to define keep-alive intervals suited to their specific energy and connectivity requirements. For instance, a battery-powered sensor in a remote agricultural field might set a relatively long keep-alive interval to conserve energy, while a mission-critical industrial sensor might set a shorter interval to ensure rapid detection of connectivity issues.

The broker's response to a PINGREQ is a PINGRESP packet, confirming that the broker is still reachable and that the session remains active. This simple two-packet exchange adds minimal overhead but significantly improves the robustness of MQTT sessions across unstable networks. If the keep-alive interval expires without communication from the client, the broker will disconnect the session and, depending on configuration, may also trigger the publication of the client's Last Will and Testament message.

The Last Will and Testament feature is another powerful capability within MQTT designed to provide system-wide awareness of unexpected client disconnections. During the initial connection handshake, the client can specify a Last Will message, along with a topic and QoS level. This message is stored by the broker and acts as a contingency for ungraceful disconnections. If the client closes the connection properly by sending a DISCONNECT packet, the broker discards the stored Last Will message. However, if the client's connection is terminated abruptly—whether due to network failure, power outage, or system crash—the broker automatically publishes the Last Will message to the designated topic on behalf of the disconnected client.

This feature is critical in systems where knowing the real-time availability of devices is essential for operational continuity and reliability. In a fleet management scenario, a vehicle's telematics unit might publish its Last Will message to a topic such as fleet/vehicle123/status with a payload indicating that the device is offline. This allows monitoring platforms and applications to take corrective actions or alert human operators immediately. Similarly, in an industrial automation environment, machinery controllers or critical sensors can publish Last Will messages to notify supervisory systems when a component goes offline unexpectedly, enabling failover mechanisms or emergency shutdown procedures.

The Last Will feature complements the keep-alive mechanism by providing a clear notification path for network anomalies and system failures. While the keep-alive mechanism is focused on maintaining active session health, the Last Will feature is about broadcasting failure states in a proactive and systematic way. The payload of a Last Will message can be fully customized, containing structured data such as JSON or XML, simple status codes, or human-readable messages, depending on the needs of the receiving applications and services.

Because Last Will messages are published by the broker as regular MQTT messages, they follow the same routing and QoS rules as any other message. This means they will only be delivered to subscribers that are actively listening to the specified topic, and they will be handled in accordance with the QoS level defined during the initial connection. Retained flag settings can also be applied to Last Will messages, allowing the broker to store the notification for future subscribers who come online after the disconnection event has occurred.

Security considerations are also important when configuring Last Will messages. Since these messages can reveal device availability or operational status, it is crucial to ensure that only authorized clients have access to the relevant topics. Access control lists on the broker can restrict which devices can publish Last Will messages and which clients can subscribe to topics associated with failure notifications. When paired with encrypted connections using TLS and strong authentication mechanisms, the Last Will system remains both secure and effective in sensitive applications.

The flexibility of the Last Will and keep-alive mechanisms means they are applicable across a wide variety of IoT use cases, from smart cities and energy grids to logistics platforms and healthcare monitoring systems. These features enable MQTT to provide an additional layer of resilience and transparency in distributed architectures, reducing downtime, improving system observability, and allowing operators to respond quickly to adverse conditions. Through the combined functionality of keep-alive intervals and Last Will messages, MQTT helps developers build systems that not only maintain persistent connections but also react intelligently and automatically to network and device failures.

MQTT Payloads and Message Formats

The payload is the core of every MQTT message, carrying the actual data that is exchanged between publishers and subscribers. Unlike other communication protocols that enforce a strict data format, MQTT is highly flexible when it comes to payload structure. The protocol itself is transport-agnostic regarding the payload, meaning it does not interpret, validate, or restrict the content in any way. From the MQTT perspective, the payload is simply a sequence of bytes attached to a PUBLISH packet. This design choice gives developers complete freedom to select the data formats and encoding methods that best suit their specific application requirements, allowing MQTT to be adapted to a wide variety of use cases and industries.

At the simplest level, an MQTT payload can be a plain text string. This is common in lightweight applications where devices need to send basic information such as status codes, single numeric values, or short alerts. For example, a smart switch may publish the string ON or OFF to represent its state. Similarly, a temperature sensor might send a simple numeric value like 24.7 to indicate the current reading in degrees Celsius. Using plain text payloads can make debugging easier and reduces complexity on resource-constrained devices, which may lack the processing power to serialize or parse more complex data structures.

However, as IoT systems scale and become more sophisticated, there is often a need for richer data representation. This has led many developers to use structured formats like JSON, XML, or even more compact binary encodings such as Protocol Buffers (Protobuf), MessagePack, or CBOR (Concise Binary Object Representation) in MQTT payloads. JSON is particularly popular due to its human-readable syntax, ease of use, and widespread support across programming languages. A payload formatted as JSON might look like {"temperature": 24.7, "humidity": 55, "unit": "C"}. This structure allows multiple data points to be transmitted in a single message, which can simplify communication and reduce the total number of messages required to represent the state of a device.

XML is another option for structured payloads, although its verbosity often makes it less attractive for bandwidth-constrained networks. XML may still be used in legacy systems or in applications where XML-based standards are mandated. In contrast, binary serialization formats like Protobuf and MessagePack provide much smaller payload sizes and faster parsing times, which are ideal for environments where every byte of bandwidth and every cycle of CPU time matters. These binary formats can significantly reduce the payload size compared to JSON or XML while preserving the ability to transmit complex data structures.

The choice of payload format depends heavily on the context of the IoT application. In some cases, human readability and interoperability are prioritized, leading teams to opt for JSON or XML. In other scenarios, especially on low-power, embedded devices communicating over limited networks, binary formats may be the preferred choice due to their efficiency. It is also common to encounter hybrid systems where different types of devices within the same MQTT deployment use different payload formats based on their capabilities and roles. Edge devices may communicate in Protobuf to conserve bandwidth, while backend cloud services convert the data into JSON for easy integration with user interfaces and reporting tools.

The payload itself is only one part of the overall MQTT PUBLISH message, which also includes metadata such as the topic name, QoS level, retain flag, and duplicate delivery flag. The broker does not inspect or modify the payload content; it only handles the delivery of the message according to the specified QoS and routing rules based on the topic. This separation of message content and delivery mechanics is a defining characteristic of MQTT and contributes to its modularity and simplicity.

Security considerations are an important aspect of payload design. Since MQTT does not encrypt payloads at the protocol level, sensitive information such as passwords, personal data, or proprietary business data should never be transmitted in plaintext. To secure the payload, developers often implement encryption at the application level or ensure that MQTT communication occurs over a TLS-encrypted channel. Additionally, some systems apply digital signatures to the payload content to verify authenticity and integrity on the subscriber's side.

Another key design consideration is payload size. While MQTT does not define strict limitations on payload length, most MQTT broker implementations and client libraries impose configurable maximum payload size limits to ensure system stability. Payloads that exceed these limits may be rejected by the broker or truncated, resulting in data loss or communication errors. When working with large data sets or files, it is recommended to divide the payload into smaller segments or use MQTT to transmit metadata while sending bulk data through alternative channels such as HTTP or FTP.

Payload consistency across the system is vital for interoperability and ease of maintenance. Defining and adhering to standard payload schemas, regardless of the chosen serialization format, helps ensure that all publishers and subscribers interpret the data correctly. Many organizations use schema definition languages such as JSON Schema or Protobuf's .proto files to document and validate payload structures. This practice is especially important in distributed teams or multi-vendor ecosystems, where different devices or services need to integrate seamlessly.

Message formatting conventions can also influence how payloads are handled downstream. For instance, systems designed to interface with data analytics platforms or machine learning models may require data to be sent in a specific format to streamline preprocessing. Time-series databases often benefit from receiving data points as timestamped records within the payload, enabling efficient storage and querying. In more advanced applications, payloads may include metadata fields such as device IDs, geographical coordinates, or quality indicators alongside the primary measurement or control data.

Finally, MQTT payloads can also include command messages intended to trigger actions on subscriber devices. In smart home or industrial automation scenarios, a payload might carry a command such as {"command": "activate", "target": "pump1", "duration": 30} to instruct a device to perform a specific task. In these cases, the payload format must be carefully designed to include clear instructions and any necessary parameters while allowing for future extensibility.

The flexibility of MQTT's payload handling empowers developers to create highly tailored solutions that meet the specific demands of their use cases. From simple text strings in hobbyist projects to complex binary structures in mission-critical industrial systems, MQTT's payload model accommodates a wide spectrum of applications. Understanding the trade-offs between readability, efficiency, and interoperability is essential when selecting and designing payload formats, as these choices directly impact system performance, maintainability, and security across the entire MQTT communication network.

MQTT Security Basics

As MQTT becomes a cornerstone of many IoT deployments across industries, securing MQTT communications has grown into a vital concern. MQTT was originally designed as a lightweight messaging protocol intended for low-bandwidth and high-latency networks, and while its simplicity is one of its greatest strengths, it also means that security features are not embedded directly into the protocol by default. Instead, MQTT relies on external mechanisms and configurations to ensure secure communication, protect data integrity, prevent unauthorized access, and defend against common security threats that can compromise IoT systems.

At the most basic level, securing MQTT starts with securing the communication channel between the MQTT clients and the broker. This is typically achieved by implementing Transport Layer Security, or TLS. TLS provides end-to-end encryption of the data in transit, ensuring that messages cannot be intercepted or read by unauthorized parties as they travel across public or private networks. TLS protects MQTT traffic from man-in-the-middle attacks and eavesdropping, safeguarding both the payload and metadata, including topics, QoS levels, and client identifiers. For many MQTT deployments, enabling TLS is considered a minimum requirement, especially when transmitting sensitive or proprietary data, or when operating over unsecured networks like the public internet.

Authentication is another critical component of MQTT security. Authentication ensures that only authorized clients can connect to the broker and participate in the messaging system. The most common form of MQTT authentication is username and password authentication, where the client provides its credentials within the CONNECT packet during session initiation. These credentials are then validated by the broker before access is granted. While simple, this approach can be vulnerable if the credentials are transmitted in plaintext over an unencrypted connection, underscoring the importance of using TLS alongside basic authentication methods.

For enhanced security, many MQTT implementations leverage client-side certificates as part of a mutual TLS (mTLS) setup. In this configuration, both the broker and the client present digital certificates to verify each other's identities. Client certificates are issued by a trusted Certificate Authority (CA) and can be customized for individual devices, providing strong, certificate-based authentication. This method is particularly valuable in large-scale or high-security IoT applications where it is necessary to establish a verifiable chain of trust between devices and the broker.

In addition to authenticating clients, it is equally important to enforce authorization, which controls what authenticated clients are allowed to do within the MQTT environment. Most MQTT brokers support access control lists (ACLs) to specify the topics that a client can publish to or subscribe from. For example, a temperature sensor in a smart building might be authorized to publish data only to topics under building1/floor2/room5/temperature but restricted from subscribing to control commands or accessing topics reserved for other rooms or devices. Fine-grained ACLs help enforce the principle of least privilege, reducing the attack surface and preventing compromised devices from accessing or manipulating unrelated parts of the system.

Topic-level authorization also plays a vital role in multi-tenant environments where different clients or organizations share the same broker. By segmenting topic hierarchies and applying strict ACLs, system architects can ensure data isolation between tenants, safeguarding customer data and ensuring compliance with industry regulations related to data privacy and security.

MQTT brokers themselves must also be secured. A broker exposed to the public internet without proper safeguards can be vulnerable to denial-of-service (DoS) attacks, brute force login attempts, or exploitation of misconfigured settings. It is common practice to place MQTT brokers behind firewalls, limit access to only trusted IP ranges, and employ intrusion detection or prevention systems to monitor for suspicious activity. In many deployments, brokers are also configured to limit the maximum number of client connections, message rates, or payload sizes to prevent resource exhaustion attacks that could degrade or shut down the service.

Beyond protecting the communication channel and broker, securing the MQTT clients is equally essential. Many IoT devices are physically accessible, making them susceptible to tampering, reverse engineering, or credential theft. Best practices for client security include hardening the device's operating system, encrypting local storage to protect credentials, disabling unused services or ports, and ensuring that firmware is kept up to date with security patches. Some IoT applications also integrate hardware security modules or trusted platform modules to store cryptographic keys securely and prevent unauthorized access at the hardware level.

Another area of concern is ensuring message integrity and authenticity. In addition to encrypting data in transit with TLS, developers may choose to implement message-level signing, where each payload includes a cryptographic signature or hash. This allows subscribers to verify that the message has not been tampered with during transit and that it was indeed sent by a trusted client. This layer of protection is useful in scenarios where messages pass through intermediaries or are stored before processing.

Monitoring and auditing are also key to maintaining a secure MQTT deployment. Many brokers support logging features that record connection attempts, subscription requests, published messages, and authentication failures. Regularly reviewing these logs helps system administrators detect unusual patterns or signs of attempted intrusions. In highly regulated industries such as finance or healthcare, maintaining detailed audit trails is often a compliance requirement, ensuring that security events can be investigated thoroughly if necessary.

Security in MQTT also extends to the proper handling of Last Will and Testament (LWT) messages. Since LWT messages often indicate that a device has unexpectedly gone offline, publishing them to secure topics and limiting who can subscribe to these topics prevents malicious actors from gaining insights into system failures or network status, which could be exploited for further attacks.

Finally, MQTT deployments should always be approached with a defense-in-depth strategy, combining multiple layers of security. This means securing the transport layer with TLS, enforcing strong client authentication and authorization policies, applying endpoint security best practices, and configuring the broker with appropriate limits and monitoring tools. By addressing security comprehensively at every level of the MQTT stack, organizations can deploy IoT solutions that are resilient against evolving cybersecurity threats while protecting the integrity, confidentiality, and availability of their data.

In summary, while MQTT's simplicity and flexibility have made it a leading protocol for IoT messaging, securing an MQTT environment requires thoughtful planning and implementation of industry-standard security practices. By focusing on transport security, authentication, authorization, broker hardening, and client protection, system designers can build secure and reliable systems capable of operating safely in both private and public networks.

Authentication and Authorization in MQTT

Authentication and authorization are two foundational components that underpin the security and integrity of MQTT-based communication systems. As MQTT is widely used across diverse environments such as smart cities, industrial automation, healthcare, and connected vehicles, ensuring that only trusted devices and applications participate in the network is critical. MQTT by design is a lightweight protocol, and while it does not mandate specific security mechanisms at the protocol level, it provides the flexibility to implement robust authentication and authorization strategies tailored to the specific needs of any deployment.

Authentication in MQTT refers to the process of verifying the identity of a client attempting to connect to a broker. Without authentication, any device or service could potentially connect to the broker, publish malicious messages, or intercept data intended for legitimate subscribers. The most basic form of authentication supported by MQTT is username and password-based authentication. During the connection handshake, when a client sends the CONNECT packet to the broker, it can include optional fields for a username and password. The broker validates these credentials against its configured authentication backend, which might be a local user database, an LDAP directory, or a cloud-based identity management system. If the credentials are incorrect or missing when required, the broker will reject the connection with an appropriate CONNACK response code.

While username and password authentication is simple and easy to implement, it also comes with limitations. Password-based authentication can be vulnerable to brute force attacks or credential leakage if not combined with additional security measures. It is recommended that passwords be complex and stored securely using hashing algorithms on the broker side. More importantly, the transmission of credentials must be protected using TLS to prevent interception during network transit. Relying solely on username and password authentication may be sufficient for small-scale or non-critical applications, but it is generally not adequate for systems where high security is a priority.

To address these limitations, many MQTT deployments opt for stronger client authentication mechanisms, such as X.509 certificates used in mutual TLS (mTLS) authentication. In this approach, both the client and the broker present digital certificates issued by a trusted certificate authority (CA) to authenticate each other during the TLS handshake. The broker validates the client certificate's signature, expiration date, and revocation status before granting access. This form of authentication not only ensures that the client is genuine but also creates an encrypted and trusted communication channel. Certificate-based authentication is particularly effective in large-scale IoT environments, where thousands of devices must be securely identified and managed across distributed systems.

Beyond client certificates, other modern authentication methods are sometimes integrated with MQTT brokers. OAuth 2.0 tokens, JSON Web Tokens (JWTs), and API keys are commonly used in cloud-native deployments where MQTT brokers are integrated into larger identity and access management (IAM) systems. These tokens allow for centralized identity management and can include metadata such as expiration times, scopes, and audience claims, giving administrators greater control over authentication policies. In these scenarios, MQTT brokers often implement custom authentication plugins or bridge with third-party services to validate the tokens before allowing clients to connect.

Authorization, distinct from authentication, governs what actions an authenticated client is allowed to perform. Once a client's identity has been verified, the broker must ensure that the client can only access resources it has been explicitly permitted to use. In MQTT, authorization typically revolves around controlling which topics a client can publish to and which topics it can subscribe from. Access control lists (ACLs) are the most widely used mechanism to enforce these policies. ACLs define rules that associate specific clients, user roles, or certificate attributes with topic-level permissions.

For instance, an ACL might grant a smart thermostat client permission to publish to home/livingroom/temperature but restrict it from publishing to home/livingroom/doorlock or subscribing to sensitive topics like home/alarm/control. By implementing ACLs at the broker level, administrators ensure that devices cannot inadvertently or maliciously publish or subscribe to topics outside of their intended scope. This prevents common security issues such as data leakage, unauthorized control commands, or cross-tenant data access in multi-tenant environments.

Authorization models can be highly granular, enabling control down to specific topic filters and wildcard levels. For example, a client could be allowed to subscribe to all topics under home/kitchen/# but denied access to home/kitchen/camera/#. Some brokers extend these capabilities by supporting dynamic authorization based on contextual parameters, such as IP address whitelisting, time-of-day restrictions, or geolocation.

In enterprise-grade deployments, authorization is often integrated with external systems such as LDAP directories, OAuth scopes, or cloud IAM roles. These integrations allow for centralized policy management and ensure that topic access aligns with broader organizational security requirements. Additionally, many modern MQTT brokers support role-based access control (RBAC), where clients are assigned roles such as publisher, subscriber, or admin, with each role defining its own set of allowed actions and topic permissions.

Securing the authentication and authorization mechanisms also requires operational best practices. For authentication, this includes rotating credentials regularly, enforcing strong password policies, and maintaining secure storage of private keys and certificates on both clients and brokers. For authorization, administrators should regularly audit ACL rules, minimize the use of wildcards where possible, and follow the principle of least privilege, granting clients only the minimum access required to perform their intended functions.

Proper logging and monitoring further enhance security in MQTT systems. Most brokers can log authentication attempts, failed login events, unauthorized access attempts, and abnormal client behaviors. Reviewing these logs helps identify potential security breaches or misconfigurations before they escalate into larger incidents. Coupled with real-time monitoring tools, alerts can be configured to notify system administrators of suspicious activities, such as repeated authentication failures from the same IP address or attempts to publish to unauthorized topics.

Ultimately, robust authentication and authorization mechanisms are essential for building secure, resilient MQTT deployments. By combining identity verification with strict access control policies, organizations can prevent unauthorized devices from infiltrating the network, protect sensitive data from leakage, and ensure that IoT systems operate as intended even under adverse conditions. As MQTT continues to power increasingly complex and mission-critical IoT ecosystems, effective authentication and authorization practices will remain central to maintaining trust, privacy, and operational integrity across all layers of the communication stack.

TLS and Secure MQTT Connections

Securing MQTT communications is a critical priority in modern IoT deployments, where sensitive data travels between millions of connected devices, edge gateways, cloud servers, and user applications. MQTT, by design, is a simple and lightweight protocol that focuses on efficiency and flexibility. However, this simplicity means that security is not embedded within the core specification of MQTT itself. To ensure confidentiality, integrity, and authenticity of the data exchanged over MQTT, the most common and effective strategy is to secure the communication channel using Transport Layer Security, or TLS.

TLS is a widely adopted cryptographic protocol that provides end-to-end encryption between communicating parties. When MQTT operates over TLS, every packet sent between the client and the broker is encrypted, protecting it from eavesdropping, man-in-the-middle attacks, and tampering. Without TLS, MQTT traffic, including payload data, topics, client IDs, and even authentication credentials like usernames and passwords, would travel over the network in plaintext. In unsecured networks, such as public Wi-Fi or mobile data networks, this leaves MQTT sessions vulnerable to interception and exploitation by malicious actors.

Implementing TLS within an MQTT system begins with configuring both the broker and the clients to support encrypted connections. Brokers typically listen on port 8883 for TLS-secured connections, which is the official IANA-assigned port for MQTT over TLS. Clients, in turn, must be configured to initiate connections to this port and provide the necessary cryptographic parameters to establish a secure session. During the TLS handshake process, the broker presents its digital certificate, which is signed by a trusted Certificate Authority (CA). The client verifies the certificate to ensure that it is communicating with a legitimate broker, mitigating the risk of connecting to a spoofed or rogue broker.

Clients may also be configured to validate the broker's hostname against the Common Name (CN) or Subject Alternative Name (SAN) fields of the certificate to prevent impersonation attacks. In this way, the combination of TLS encryption and certificate validation provides strong assurances that data is being transmitted securely and only to intended recipients. Once the handshake is completed, all MQTT messages are transmitted within the encrypted tunnel, shielding them from any unauthorized inspection.

In addition to securing the communication channel, TLS can also be configured for mutual authentication, commonly known as mutual TLS or mTLS. In an mTLS setup, not only does the broker present a certificate to the client, but the client also presents its own certificate back to the broker. This mutual exchange establishes bidirectional trust, where both parties verify each other's identities. mTLS is particularly valuable in IoT ecosystems with strict security requirements, where individual devices must be strongly authenticated before being allowed to publish or subscribe to topics.

Deploying mTLS involves generating and managing client certificates, which are typically issued by an internal or public CA. These certificates are securely installed on client devices and are often linked to unique identifiers, such as device serial numbers or cryptographic hardware modules, to provide traceable and tamper-resistant identity verification. Once configured, mTLS significantly enhances the security posture of the system by eliminating reliance on simple passwords or API keys, which can be more easily compromised or misused.

While TLS provides strong encryption, proper configuration is essential to ensure maximum security. It is important to enforce the use of up-to-date and secure versions of the TLS protocol, such as TLS 1.2 or TLS 1.3, while disabling older, less secure versions like SSLv3 or TLS 1.0, which are vulnerable to known exploits. The selection of cipher suites also plays a crucial role. Strong ciphers that support Perfect Forward Secrecy (PFS), such as those using Elliptic Curve Diffie-Hellman Ephemeral (ECDHE) key exchange, are recommended to protect past communications even if long-term private keys are compromised in the future.

Additionally, it is best practice to implement certificate revocation mechanisms, such as Certificate Revocation Lists (CRLs) or the Online Certificate Status Protocol (OCSP), to ensure that compromised or expired certificates are promptly invalidated. Regularly rotating server and client certificates further enhances security and helps reduce the window of opportunity for attackers in the event of key compromise.

TLS does introduce some trade-offs, particularly in resource-constrained environments common in IoT. The encryption and decryption processes add computational overhead and can increase latency, which may be a consideration for ultra-low-power devices or systems with stringent real-time requirements. To address this, developers often optimize TLS libraries for embedded systems, choosing lightweight cryptographic algorithms and minimizing handshake operations through session resumption techniques. Despite the overhead, the benefits of securing MQTT traffic with TLS far outweigh the performance costs, especially when dealing with sensitive data such as health records, financial information, or critical infrastructure telemetry.

TLS is also essential when MQTT is deployed over public cloud platforms, where data frequently traverses the open internet. Leading cloud providers such as Amazon Web Services (AWS), Microsoft Azure, and Google Cloud all require or strongly recommend the use of TLS for MQTT endpoints. Cloud-hosted MQTT brokers often integrate TLS with additional security features like IAM-based authentication, firewall configurations, and audit logging, further strengthening the security perimeter of the system.

Securing MQTT connections with TLS also complements other MQTT security practices, such as implementing access control lists, session management, and monitoring tools. Even with TLS in place, unauthorized access to topics or services could occur if proper broker-side authorization policies are not enforced. Therefore, TLS should always be viewed as a foundational security layer to be combined with strong identity verification and topic-level access controls.

Finally, system designers must also address operational aspects of TLS, such as secure key storage and certificate management automation. Client devices should store private keys in secure enclaves or hardware security modules to prevent extraction and misuse. In large deployments with thousands or millions of devices, leveraging certificate management platforms and automated provisioning workflows simplifies the process of issuing, renewing, and revoking certificates.

TLS has become the industry-standard method of securing MQTT communication channels, ensuring confidentiality, integrity, and authentication across a wide range of IoT applications. By encrypting all MQTT traffic and verifying endpoint identities through digital certificates, TLS fortifies the protocol against common network threats and creates a secure foundation for building reliable and trustworthy IoT solutions. Whether used in small-scale smart home networks or vast industrial IoT deployments, TLS is indispensable to modern MQTT security architectures.

MQTT Over WebSockets

The ability to run MQTT over WebSockets has expanded the versatility and reach of the protocol, allowing MQTT clients to communicate effectively across modern web architectures and browser-based environments. Traditionally, MQTT operates over TCP/IP, which is suitable for embedded systems, servers, and backend applications. However, as the Internet of Things began merging with web technologies and cloud-native platforms, there emerged a need to bridge MQTT's messaging capabilities with web applications, dashboards, and browser-based user interfaces. WebSockets provide that bridge, enabling MQTT to function seamlessly over HTTP infrastructure while maintaining its efficient publish-subscribe model.

WebSockets are a communication protocol designed to provide full-duplex, persistent connections over a single TCP connection. They are initiated as an HTTP request and then upgraded to a WebSocket connection, making them highly compatible with firewalls, proxies, and load balancers that are commonly found in enterprise networks and cloud services. Because WebSockets start as HTTP, they can traverse environments where traditional MQTT traffic on TCP port 1883 might be blocked, but HTTP ports like 80 and 443 are open and widely accepted. This flexibility has made MQTT over WebSockets a favored solution for integrating real-time messaging into web-based frontends and other systems reliant on standard web technologies.

When MQTT runs over WebSockets, the fundamental publish-subscribe model of MQTT remains unchanged. Clients still connect to a broker, publish messages to topics, and subscribe to topics of interest. The key difference is that instead of establishing a direct TCP connection to the broker's native MQTT port, the client initiates a WebSocket handshake with the broker's HTTP or HTTPS port. Once the handshake completes and the connection is upgraded to a WebSocket, MQTT control packets are transmitted within the WebSocket frames. This encapsulation allows MQTT to piggyback on existing web protocols without losing the advantages of its lightweight design and asynchronous communication model.

One of the most significant use cases for MQTT over WebSockets is in web-based dashboards and IoT control panels. For instance, a smart building management system might feature a web interface where facility managers can monitor sensor readings, receive alerts, or control devices remotely. Using WebSockets, the browser acts as a fully functional MQTT client, subscribing to topics such as building1/floor2/temperature or building1/floor3/occupancy. These messages are delivered in real-time to the browser, allowing operators to see live updates and control devices directly from a web interface without the need for constant HTTP polling or page refreshes.

The use of MQTT over WebSockets is also common in mobile applications, where developers leverage standard web libraries and frameworks to interact with MQTT brokers. Libraries such as Eclipse Paho, MQTT.js, and other JavaScript-based MQTT clients offer built-in support for WebSockets, making it easy to integrate MQTT communication into web or hybrid mobile applications. This enables a broad range of real-time IoT use cases, from fleet management apps displaying live vehicle telemetry to home automation apps that allow users to adjust smart thermostats or view security camera feeds.

Securing MQTT over WebSockets is typically done using WebSocket Secure (WSS), which layers WebSockets over HTTPS. When WSS is employed, all MQTT packets encapsulated within the WebSocket frames are transmitted over an encrypted TLS tunnel, providing the same level of security as traditional MQTT over TLS on port 8883. This ensures that data transmitted between browsers or web clients and the broker is protected against interception, tampering, and eavesdropping. As with standard WebSocket connections, brokers using WSS typically operate on port 443, making them compatible with strict firewall rules and content delivery networks (CDNs).

Running MQTT over WebSockets does introduce some additional overhead compared to native MQTT over TCP. The WebSocket framing adds slight latency and increases packet size due to encapsulation. However, this trade-off is often acceptable in scenarios where browser compatibility and firewall traversal are more important than minimizing every byte of overhead. In many real-world applications, the latency introduced by WebSocket encapsulation is negligible compared to the benefits of seamless integration with web technologies.

Configuring MQTT over WebSockets requires both broker-side and client-side adjustments. On the broker side, MQTT brokers such as Eclipse Mosquitto, EMQX, HiveMQ, and AWS IoT Core support WebSocket listeners alongside standard TCP listeners. Administrators must enable the WebSocket service and configure the broker to accept incoming WebSocket connections, often specifying allowed origins, SSL certificates, and access control rules. On the client side, developers specify the WebSocket URI, such as wss://broker.example.com/mqtt, when creating the client instance. Once connected, the MQTT session behaves identically to a standard session, supporting the full range of MQTT features including Quality of Service (QoS) levels, retained messages, Last Will and Testament, and topic hierarchies.

Beyond browser integration, MQTT over WebSockets is also useful in serverless and cloud-native applications. Modern cloud platforms increasingly favor HTTP-based interfaces for scalability and flexibility. WebSockets allow MQTT to integrate with serverless functions, microservices, and API gateways that might not support traditional MQTT TCP traffic. For example, a serverless function could act as an MQTT client over WebSockets, subscribing to specific topics and triggering business logic when messages are received, without needing a dedicated MQTT client library tied to a TCP-based transport.

In addition, MQTT over WebSockets is advantageous for real-time analytics and event-driven architectures. WebSocket-based MQTT clients can feed live data streams directly into web applications for visualization or into cloud-native event processing pipelines for immediate analysis. This enables organizations to build responsive systems where users or applications receive actionable insights with minimal delay.

In the context of hybrid systems, MQTT over WebSockets often coexists alongside native MQTT over TCP. Devices such as sensors and embedded systems might connect directly over TCP to minimize overhead and optimize battery life, while user interfaces and mobile apps connect via WebSockets for accessibility. This hybrid approach allows IoT architects to select the most appropriate transport mechanism based on device capabilities and network environments, creating a versatile and adaptable architecture.

While MQTT over WebSockets brings significant advantages for specific scenarios, developers must also be mindful of scalability and broker resource consumption. Handling large numbers of WebSocket connections can require careful tuning of broker parameters, network infrastructure, and load balancing strategies. Using tools like WebSocket connection limits, HTTP/2 multiplexing, or CDN-based acceleration can help optimize performance in high-traffic deployments.

The combination of MQTT's efficient messaging model with the compatibility and reach of WebSockets has enabled new classes of applications that blend IoT and web technologies. MQTT over WebSockets has become an essential tool in the development of modern IoT systems where accessibility, real-time interaction, and cross-platform compatibility are key drivers of success. Whether powering interactive dashboards, cloud-native services, or mobile apps, this approach expands the possibilities for delivering MQTT-based messaging to a broader range of users and devices.

MQTT and Cloud Platforms

The convergence of MQTT and cloud platforms has transformed the way organizations design and deploy IoT systems. While MQTT was originally designed as a lightweight protocol for constrained devices and unreliable networks, its adoption has expanded dramatically with the rise of cloud computing. Modern IoT systems often involve thousands or even millions of devices transmitting data to centralized cloud services for processing, analysis, and storage. MQTT has become a critical enabler of this architecture, offering a scalable and efficient messaging solution that integrates seamlessly with major cloud platforms.

Cloud providers such as Amazon Web Services (AWS), Microsoft Azure, Google Cloud Platform (GCP), and IBM Cloud have each developed managed MQTT broker services that abstract much of the operational complexity involved in running and maintaining MQTT infrastructure. These managed services eliminate the need for organizations to deploy and manage their own brokers on virtual machines or dedicated servers, providing a fully managed, secure, and highly available MQTT environment. This allows companies to focus more on developing applications and services rather than worrying about broker maintenance, scaling issues, or system uptime.

One of the primary advantages of using MQTT on cloud platforms is the ability to scale effortlessly with demand. Traditional on-premises MQTT brokers may struggle under the weight of thousands of simultaneous client connections or heavy message throughput without careful tuning or clustering. Cloud platforms, on the other hand, offer elastic scaling, automatically provisioning additional resources as the load increases. For example, AWS IoT Core can handle millions of connected devices, scaling behind the scenes to ensure reliable message delivery and low latency even during periods of high traffic. This scalability is critical for large-scale deployments, such as smart cities, industrial IoT networks, or global supply chain monitoring systems.

Security is another key benefit when using MQTT with cloud services. Managed cloud-based MQTT brokers are typically integrated with the provider's broader security ecosystem, offering features such as fine-grained access control, TLS encryption by default, and robust authentication mechanisms. For instance, AWS IoT Core integrates with AWS Identity and Access Management (IAM) to enforce permissions on a per-client or per-topic basis, while Azure IoT Hub uses role-based access control (RBAC) and integrates with Azure Active Directory. These integrations allow administrators to apply enterprise-grade security policies and practices to MQTT communications, including rotating credentials, enforcing least privilege, and integrating with existing identity management workflows.

Cloud platforms also enable tighter integration between MQTT messaging and other cloud-native services, such as data lakes, databases, machine learning services, and analytics pipelines. When a device publishes a message to a topic, the broker can trigger downstream workflows, including serverless functions, event hubs, or streaming services. For example, in AWS IoT Core, messages can be routed directly to AWS Lambda functions for processing or transformation before being stored in Amazon S3, ingested into Amazon Kinesis for real-time analytics, or forwarded to Amazon DynamoDB for structured storage. In Google Cloud, messages from Cloud IoT Core's MQTT bridge can flow into Google Cloud Pub/Sub, allowing developers to build event-driven architectures that process IoT data at scale.

These integrations reduce the complexity of building end-to-end IoT solutions, enabling organizations to develop systems where devices in the field seamlessly communicate with backend applications and data pipelines. MQTT becomes the messaging backbone, carrying telemetry data, device status updates, or remote control commands between edge devices and cloud-hosted applications. This helps accelerate time to market, simplifies system maintenance, and fosters innovation across industries.

Another important factor driving MQTT adoption in the cloud is global reach. Cloud platforms operate data centers across multiple geographic regions, allowing MQTT deployments to be distributed closer to the edge where devices are located. This reduces latency and improves system responsiveness. For instance, a multinational company with devices deployed across North America, Europe, and Asia can leverage regionally distributed brokers offered by their chosen cloud provider, ensuring that messages are delivered quickly and efficiently to the nearest broker endpoint.

Additionally, cloud platforms often offer MQTT over WebSockets support, facilitating seamless integration with web applications and browser-based user interfaces. This capability enables developers to build dashboards, monitoring tools, and control panels that receive real-time data streams directly from the cloud broker without relying on intermediate systems. Operators and end-users can interact with IoT data in real time via secure web interfaces, improving decision-making and operational awareness.

Many cloud platforms also provide advanced monitoring and observability tools for MQTT traffic. Administrators can view metrics such as message throughput, connection counts, error rates, and latency directly through cloud-native dashboards. These monitoring tools make it easier to detect anomalies, troubleshoot communication issues, and optimize system performance. Alerts and automated responses can be configured to respond to specific conditions, such as an unexpected drop in the number of connected devices or a spike in undelivered messages.

Cloud-hosted MQTT brokers also benefit from high availability and disaster recovery features inherent in cloud infrastructure. Managed MQTT services are typically deployed across multiple availability zones, ensuring resilience against regional outages or hardware failures. Service-level agreements (SLAs) provided by cloud vendors guarantee uptime and reliability, reducing the operational burden on organizations to build and manage highly available MQTT broker clusters manually.

For organizations looking to integrate legacy systems or hybrid cloud-edge architectures, cloud platforms support MQTT bridging and gateway solutions. Edge gateways deployed on-premises can aggregate local device data via MQTT and forward it to cloud brokers securely, enabling seamless data synchronization between edge and cloud environments. This is particularly useful in industrial settings, where real-time decision-making is handled locally at the edge while aggregated data is forwarded to the cloud for historical analysis and business intelligence.

Furthermore, cloud providers are increasingly offering SDKs, APIs, and pre-built components that simplify the integration of MQTT clients into IoT devices. These development tools support a variety of programming languages and hardware platforms, making it easier for developers to implement MQTT communication across a diverse set of devices, from microcontrollers to embedded Linux systems and containerized applications.

The combination of MQTT's lightweight protocol design with the power and flexibility of cloud platforms has enabled new possibilities in IoT system design. From smart agriculture to connected healthcare and smart energy grids, MQTT over cloud infrastructure delivers the scalability, security, and agility needed to support a wide range of use cases. It bridges the gap between resource-constrained edge devices and the sophisticated analytics, storage, and orchestration services available in modern cloud environments.

Ultimately, leveraging MQTT with cloud platforms empowers organizations to unlock the full potential of their IoT deployments, streamlining operations, reducing infrastructure costs, and creating the foundation for scalable, intelligent, and globally connected systems.

MQTT on Resource-Constrained Devices

The growing presence of MQTT in the IoT landscape is largely due to its ability to function effectively on resource-constrained devices. These devices, which include microcontrollers, embedded systems, battery-powered sensors, and simple actuators, often operate with limited processing power, memory, storage capacity, and energy reserves. In many IoT scenarios, these devices are deployed in remote, harsh, or mobile environments, where network reliability may be intermittent, and power efficiency is critical. MQTT's lightweight nature and efficient publish-subscribe communication model make it particularly well-suited for these challenging conditions.

Resource-constrained devices typically rely on microcontrollers such as ARM Cortex-M, AVR, ESP32, or similar low-power chips. These devices may only have a few hundred kilobytes of RAM and minimal flash storage, yet they need to handle communication tasks, process sensor data, and maintain secure connections with centralized systems. MQTT, with its minimal packet overhead and low computational demands, allows these devices to participate in networked systems without requiring high-end hardware. Its compact control packet structure, which can consist of as little as two bytes in the fixed header for certain operations, helps minimize the impact on system resources.

One of the primary benefits of MQTT on constrained devices is its efficiency in terms of bandwidth usage. Many of these devices operate over low-power and low-bandwidth communication links such as LoRaWAN, NB-IoT, Zigbee, or narrowband cellular networks, where reducing the amount of data transmitted is crucial for maintaining battery life and minimizing operational costs. MQTT's small message footprint and ability to handle simple payloads with minimal protocol overhead help conserve bandwidth, making it ideal for sending telemetry data such as temperature readings, humidity levels, motion detection events, or GPS coordinates.

The publish-subscribe architecture of MQTT also aligns well with the communication patterns of resource-limited devices. Rather than maintaining persistent connections with multiple peer devices or relying on request-response models that require higher energy consumption and more complex logic, these devices simply publish data to a broker and disconnect or remain idle until necessary. The broker handles message distribution, eliminating the need for devices to manage multiple direct connections, further conserving processing and memory resources.

Power efficiency is another area where MQTT excels in constrained environments. Devices that rely on batteries or energy-harvesting methods must minimize energy consumption to extend their operational lifespan. MQTT allows for flexible connection strategies to achieve this. Some devices establish a connection, publish data, and disconnect immediately, reducing radio-on time and conserving power. Others may leverage MQTT's persistent session feature, allowing the broker to queue messages and deliver them once the device reconnects. This is particularly important for sensors that operate in deep-sleep modes, waking up periodically to transmit data and then returning to a low-power state.

MQTT's Quality of Service levels are also beneficial for optimizing resource usage on constrained devices. While QoS 2 offers exactly once delivery guarantees, most resource-constrained devices use QoS 0 or QoS 1. QoS 0, or at most once delivery, is the most lightweight option and is often sufficient when occasional message loss is acceptable or when data redundancy exists, such as in frequent sensor reporting. QoS 1, or at least once delivery, adds a minimal acknowledgment mechanism that provides a balance between reliability and resource usage, making it a common choice for applications where message delivery assurance is important but system resources are still limited.

To run MQTT on microcontrollers and embedded systems, developers often rely on lightweight MQTT client libraries specifically designed for constrained environments. Libraries such as Eclipse Paho Embedded, Eclipse MQTTC, or the Arduino PubSubClient library are optimized for microcontrollers, offering minimal memory footprints and simplified APIs. These libraries provide core MQTT functionality, such as connecting to brokers, publishing and subscribing to topics, and handling keep-alive intervals, while omitting features that might introduce unnecessary overhead for devices with limited capabilities.

The ability to integrate MQTT into constrained devices also depends on the efficiency of the underlying transport layer. MQTT is typically implemented over TCP/IP, but TCP can be challenging for very low-power devices due to its connection-oriented nature and overhead. However, in many embedded systems, lightweight TCP/IP stacks such as lwIP or uIP provide stripped-down versions of the protocol that minimize memory usage while maintaining compliance with IP-based communication standards. In some use cases, constrained devices rely on gateway nodes that act as MQTT clients on their behalf, aggregating sensor data via non-IP protocols such as SPI, I2C, or UART, and then relaying it to the broker over TCP/IP.

Security on constrained devices poses additional challenges, as encryption algorithms and secure transport protocols can be computationally demanding. Nevertheless, many MQTT implementations on resource-limited devices support TLS through libraries optimized for embedded systems, such as mbed TLS or WolfSSL. While using TLS does consume additional memory and processing cycles, it is often necessary when transmitting sensitive data or when connecting to cloud-based brokers that mandate encrypted connections. Some devices may offload encryption tasks to hardware accelerators, reducing the burden on the main microcontroller.

In highly constrained environments where TLS is not feasible, developers may implement lightweight alternatives, such as pre-shared keys or message-level encryption using simple cryptographic algorithms. However, these solutions require careful design to avoid introducing vulnerabilities. Device identity management is also streamlined for constrained systems, with client authentication often relying on simple tokens, unique device IDs, or lightweight certificate formats.

MQTT's adaptability is further demonstrated in its ability to coexist with real-time operating systems (RTOS) frequently used in constrained devices. RTOS platforms such as FreeRTOS, Zephyr, and RIOT OS offer lightweight scheduling and task management, enabling MQTT clients to run alongside other application logic without exhausting system resources. MQTT client tasks can be configured to operate as low-priority background services or as periodic jobs that activate only when network communication is necessary.

In mission-critical applications such as remote environmental monitoring, industrial automation, and precision agriculture, the combination of MQTT and constrained devices has unlocked the potential for large-scale sensor networks that operate autonomously for months or years at a time. These systems deliver valuable data to centralized platforms while minimizing maintenance costs and power consumption. As hardware advances continue to reduce the power and size of microcontrollers, and as energy-efficient wireless technologies proliferate, MQTT will remain a key enabler of communication in the growing ecosystem of resource-constrained IoT devices.

MQTT for Industrial IoT Applications

Industrial IoT, often referred to as IIoT, represents a critical segment within the larger Internet of Things ecosystem, focusing on enhancing the efficiency, safety, and automation of industrial processes. MQTT has emerged as a preferred protocol for IIoT systems, due to its ability to handle machine-to-machine communication in environments where reliability, low bandwidth, and low latency are essential. Industries such as manufacturing, energy, transportation, and utilities have increasingly adopted MQTT to connect sensors, controllers, machinery, and cloud-based applications, creating highly responsive and intelligent industrial networks.

One of the key reasons MQTT excels in industrial settings is its publish-subscribe architecture, which allows devices to communicate asynchronously and in a decoupled manner. This approach contrasts with traditional client-server models, where devices may need to maintain direct connections and initiate repetitive polling mechanisms. In a factory or plant floor scenario, MQTT enables multiple devices, such as programmable logic controllers (PLCs), robotic arms, and SCADA systems, to publish data to centralized brokers, while other systems and applications subscribe to relevant topics to monitor or control these devices. This results in an architecture where new equipment or systems can be easily integrated into the network without redesigning or reconfiguring the entire communication structure.

Industrial environments often consist of legacy equipment and protocols, which require seamless integration with modern IoT technologies. MQTT bridges this gap by functioning as a protocol translator between traditional fieldbus protocols, like Modbus, PROFIBUS, or OPC UA, and modern cloud-native platforms. Gateways equipped with MQTT clients aggregate data from legacy systems and publish it to MQTT brokers, where cloud services or supervisory applications can access and process it. This allows industries to leverage existing infrastructure while still benefiting from the flexibility and scalability of IoT platforms.

Another significant advantage of MQTT in IIoT applications is its low overhead and optimized bandwidth usage. Many industrial facilities operate in areas with limited or expensive connectivity, such as remote oil rigs, offshore wind farms, or mining operations. MQTT's lightweight design, with small header sizes and efficient message formatting, ensures that critical telemetry and control data can be transmitted reliably even over constrained networks like satellite links or private radio systems. This efficiency not only reduces operational costs but also extends the life of power-constrained edge devices deployed in the field.

In industrial settings, the need for reliable and deterministic communication is paramount. MQTT's support for different Quality of Service (QoS) levels allows system designers to select the appropriate delivery guarantees based on the importance of the data. For non-critical information, such as routine environmental measurements, QoS o may suffice, minimizing network usage. However, for critical control commands or safety alerts, QoS 1 or QoS 2 ensures that messages are delivered reliably, with acknowledgments and retransmissions where necessary. This capability is essential for applications like industrial automation, where machinery must respond promptly to commands to avoid production stoppages or safety incidents.

Security is also a vital concern in IIoT deployments. Industrial networks are often targets for cyber threats due to their role in controlling critical infrastructure. MQTT supports secure communication through the use of TLS encryption, ensuring that sensitive data such as equipment status, control commands, or operational metrics are protected from unauthorized interception or tampering. Many industrial applications also employ mutual TLS authentication to validate both client and broker identities, further safeguarding the system against malicious actors.

Moreover, MQTT's Last Will and Testament (LWT) feature is particularly useful in industrial applications where device health monitoring is a priority. If a sensor, actuator, or controller disconnects unexpectedly due to hardware failure, network outage, or power loss, the broker can automatically publish a predefined LWT message to notify supervisory systems and operators of the disconnection. This real-time awareness allows maintenance teams to take corrective action quickly, minimizing downtime and improving overall system resilience.

Industrial processes often involve thousands of connected devices generating vast amounts of telemetry data in real-time. MQTT supports hierarchical topic structures, which enable logical organization of messages. In a smart factory, topics might be structured as plant1/lineA/machine5/temperature or plant1/lineB/robot3/status, allowing different departments, analytics platforms, and control systems to subscribe to the specific data streams they require. The topic hierarchy simplifies message routing and filtering, ensuring that relevant data is delivered efficiently to the correct recipients without overloading the network or processing systems.

Cloud integration is a growing trend in IIoT, as industries seek to leverage advanced analytics, predictive maintenance, and artificial intelligence (AI) to optimize operations. MQTT plays a pivotal role in transmitting data from the edge, where devices reside, to cloud platforms where analytics and machine learning models are applied. By connecting plant floor devices to cloud services via MQTT, organizations can gain real-time insights into asset performance, energy usage, and production metrics, enabling data-driven decision-making and continuous process improvement.

Edge computing has further strengthened MQTT's relevance in IIoT. In many industrial scenarios, data needs to be processed locally before being transmitted to the cloud to reduce latency and conserve bandwidth. MQTT brokers deployed on local edge gateways facilitate fast and reliable communication between devices within the facility while selectively forwarding critical insights or aggregated data to remote cloud systems. This hybrid approach balances local autonomy and centralized management, making it ideal for use cases such as predictive maintenance, where real-time alerts must be issued based on immediate analysis of sensor data.

Another application of MQTT in IIoT is condition-based monitoring. Sensors embedded in machinery continuously publish vibration, temperature, pressure, or motor current data to an MQTT broker. Analytical models running at the edge or in the cloud subscribe to these topics to detect anomalies or deviations from expected patterns. If abnormal conditions are detected, such as excessive vibrations indicating impending equipment failure, alerts can be issued immediately, preventing unplanned downtime and reducing maintenance costs.

In transportation and logistics, MQTT supports fleet management solutions where vehicles, cargo containers, and transport infrastructure are interconnected. Trucks, ships, or trains equipped with MQTT clients can publish location data, cargo status, and diagnostics to central systems, enhancing visibility across supply chains and enabling predictive routing, load optimization, and maintenance planning.

The adoption of MQTT in IIoT environments has contributed to the rise of Industry 4.0, characterized by the convergence of cyber-physical systems, advanced automation, and cloud-based analytics. As industrial organizations strive to achieve smarter and more efficient operations, MQTT provides the communication backbone that bridges sensors, machines, and IT systems, delivering the responsiveness, flexibility, and scalability required in modern industrial ecosystems.

MQTT in Smart Home Ecosystems

The emergence of smart home technologies has brought about a revolution in how people interact with their living spaces, blending convenience, automation, and energy efficiency into everyday life. At the heart of many smart home ecosystems lies MQTT, a protocol that has become a de facto standard for lightweight, real-time messaging between connected devices. MQTT's publish-subscribe model, low resource requirements, and support for asynchronous communication make it a natural choice for managing the diverse range of devices that make up a modern smart home, from sensors and appliances to lighting systems and security components.

In a typical smart home environment, a variety of devices and subsystems operate together to create a unified and automated experience for the user. Devices such as thermostats, smart plugs, lighting controllers, security cameras, motion sensors, door locks, voice assistants, and HVAC systems often need to exchange information and respond to commands in real time. MQTT facilitates this by providing a communication backbone where devices publish status updates, sensor readings, and alerts to a centralized broker, while other devices and applications subscribe to these topics to take appropriate actions.

One of the key strengths of MQTT in the smart home is its ability to decouple devices from one another. Instead of requiring direct peer-to-peer communication or rigid client-server architectures, MQTT enables devices to interact indirectly through the broker. For example, a motion sensor might publish to the topic home/livingroom/motion when it detects movement. A lighting controller subscribed to that topic can then automatically turn on the lights in the living room without the motion sensor needing to know anything about the lighting system. This decoupled approach simplifies system design, reduces configuration complexity, and enhances the modularity and scalability of the smart home network.

MQTT's topic hierarchy system further enhances the organization and flexibility of smart home automation. Topics can be logically structured to mirror the physical layout of the home, such as home/kitchen/temperature, home/bedroom1/humidity, or home/garage/door/status. This allows for intuitive grouping of devices and simplifies the process of setting up automation rules or managing devices through a centralized smart home hub or cloud-based controller. Users or automation engines can subscribe to specific rooms, device types, or entire categories of sensors using wildcards. For instance, subscribing to home/+/motion allows a system to monitor motion events across all rooms without needing to subscribe to each individual topic.

Smart home ecosystems are also highly event-driven, and MQTT's asynchronous communication model aligns perfectly with this characteristic. Devices in the smart home do not always require continuous data exchange but rather respond to events, triggers, and scheduled tasks. A thermostat might adjust heating only when the temperature sensor reports that the room has fallen below a specified threshold, or a voice assistant might publish a command to home/kitchen/light/set when a user requests the kitchen lights to be dimmed. By only transmitting data when necessary, MQTT helps minimize network traffic, conserves device power, and improves the responsiveness of the overall system.

Another reason MQTT is well-suited to smart home applications is its support for resource-constrained devices. Many smart home devices, such as battery-powered sensors or Wi-Fi-enabled microcontrollers, operate with limited processing power and memory. MQTT's lightweight packet structure and efficient protocol design ensure that these devices can maintain reliable communication with minimal resource consumption. Moreover, MQTT allows devices to operate on low-bandwidth or intermittent networks without sacrificing functionality. Devices can use persistent sessions and the Last Will and

Testament feature to signal unexpected disconnections, helping smart home platforms monitor device health and provide timely alerts to users when a sensor or appliance goes offline.

Security and privacy are critical considerations in smart home deployments, where personal data and control over physical spaces are at stake. MQTT provides a foundation for secure communication by supporting Transport Layer Security (TLS), which encrypts data in transit between devices and brokers. In addition, brokers can enforce authentication using username and password combinations or client certificates to ensure that only authorized devices and applications can access or control smart home resources. Many smart home enthusiasts and commercial vendors also implement topic-level access control to limit which devices can publish to or subscribe from sensitive topics, such as home/alarm/trigger or home/doorlock/command.

Another advantage of MQTT in the smart home is its compatibility with cloud platforms and mobile applications. MQTT can operate both locally, via a broker running on a home server or smart home hub, and remotely through cloud-hosted brokers provided by services like AWS IoT Core, Azure IoT Hub, or custom deployments. This flexibility enables homeowners to control and monitor their smart home devices from anywhere in the world using smartphone apps or web dashboards that act as MQTT clients via secure cloud connections. For example, a user could check the status of their front door lock, receive alerts about water leaks, or remotely adjust their home thermostat while away from home.

MQTT's integration with voice assistants and smart home ecosystems such as Amazon Alexa, Google Home, and Apple HomeKit further enhances the user experience. Many home automation platforms bridge MQTT messages with these ecosystems, enabling users to control MQTT-connected devices using voice commands or routines. For instance, a smart speaker might trigger an MQTT message to turn off all lights at bedtime or activate security sensors when the user says a predefined phrase.

Edge computing is also increasingly being deployed in smart homes alongside MQTT to enhance automation and reduce dependency on cloud services. Smart home hubs equipped with local MQTT brokers and automation engines can process sensor data, make decisions, and execute automation logic locally, ensuring the home continues to operate even if internet connectivity is lost. This local-first approach is valued for its reliability and privacy, as data never leaves the home unless explicitly configured to do so.

In addition, MQTT's retained message feature plays a useful role in smart homes by ensuring that newly connected devices or applications immediately receive the latest status information. A lighting control panel, for example, might retrieve the current on/off state of lights via retained messages without waiting for the next state change to be published. This ensures that user interfaces and automation systems always have the most recent context available when making decisions or displaying information to occupants.

MQTT has proven itself to be a powerful enabler of flexible, scalable, and responsive smart home ecosystems. By providing a lightweight and efficient messaging protocol capable of integrating a wide variety of devices, platforms, and services, MQTT allows homeowners to create personalized, automated environments that enhance comfort, security, and energy efficiency. Whether powering simple automations like turning on hallway lights when motion is detected or orchestrating complex routines that involve multiple devices and cloud services, MQTT serves as a reliable backbone for the connected home.

MQTT in Automotive and Transportation

The automotive and transportation industries have undergone a significant transformation through the integration of connected technologies. Vehicles, infrastructure, and logistics systems are increasingly reliant on real-time data exchange to improve safety, efficiency, and customer experience. MQTT has emerged as a critical protocol supporting these connected applications due to its lightweight nature, efficient bandwidth usage, and ability to function reliably across unstable and mobile networks. Whether embedded within connected cars, fleet management systems, or public transportation networks, MQTT provides the essential communication layer that powers modern mobility solutions.

In connected vehicles, MQTT facilitates a wide range of telemetry, diagnostics, and infotainment functions. Modern cars are equipped with dozens of electronic control units (ECUs) and sensors that monitor everything from engine performance and fuel efficiency to tire pressure and environmental conditions. Using MQTT, these data points can be transmitted from the vehicle to cloud platforms or backend services for real-time monitoring and predictive maintenance. A car's telematics unit, acting as an MQTT client, may publish messages on topics such as vehicle123/engine/temperature or vehicle123/location/gps. These messages are then consumed by services that analyze vehicle health, track fleet locations, or alert operators to critical issues before they escalate.

The automotive industry places a premium on bandwidth efficiency, especially for vehicles operating in areas with intermittent or costly cellular connectivity. MQTT's minimal overhead allows it to transmit key data without placing an undue burden on available bandwidth. Since vehicles are constantly in motion and may traverse regions with poor network coverage, MQTT's publish-subscribe model is particularly advantageous. Devices within the vehicle can buffer data locally and publish it to the broker once network connectivity is restored, ensuring that no critical information is lost during disconnections. This is especially valuable for long-haul trucks, buses, or ships that may be offline for extended periods but still need to relay telemetry data to centralized systems.

Fleet management is another domain where MQTT plays an increasingly pivotal role. Logistics companies use MQTT to maintain real-time visibility into the status and performance of their fleets. MQTT clients installed on trucks, delivery vans, or service vehicles report vital information such as fuel consumption, cargo temperature, vehicle diagnostics, and driver behavior metrics to MQTT brokers hosted in data centers or cloud platforms. This constant data flow allows fleet operators to make informed decisions regarding route optimization, driver safety, maintenance scheduling, and load management. When combined with GPS data, MQTT enables real-time vehicle tracking, which is essential for improving delivery accuracy, reducing idle times, and responding proactively to unexpected events such as traffic congestion or mechanical issues.

In public transportation, MQTT supports the infrastructure required for smart city initiatives. Buses, trains, and trams equipped with MQTT clients can transmit real-time location data, passenger counts, and system status updates to transit management platforms. This information is used to optimize schedules, manage traffic flow, and provide passengers with accurate arrival and departure times through public displays or mobile apps. For example, a city's transport system might subscribe to topics such as city/transit/bus123/location or city/transit/train5/capacity to dynamically adjust resources and enhance the commuter experience.

Beyond vehicles, MQTT is increasingly deployed in traffic management systems and connected infrastructure. Traffic lights, electronic road signs, toll booths, and parking meters are outfitted with IoT sensors and control units that utilize MQTT to share status updates, usage statistics, and fault reports with centralized control centers. This data enables city planners and operators to implement adaptive traffic control strategies, reduce congestion, and improve urban mobility. For instance, traffic cameras and vehicle counters might publish messages to a broker, allowing traffic signals to automatically adjust their timing based on real-time traffic density.

Another growing use case is vehicle-to-infrastructure (V2I) and vehicle-to-everything (V2X) communication, which form the foundation for autonomous and semi-autonomous vehicle systems. In V2I scenarios, connected cars use MQTT to receive and act upon information from surrounding infrastructure, such as road hazard warnings, construction zone alerts, or dynamic speed limits. These messages may be published by roadside units or centralized transportation systems, providing drivers and autonomous driving algorithms with the situational awareness required to make safer and more efficient driving decisions. Similarly, in V2X networks, vehicles, infrastructure, pedestrians, and other road users communicate with one another through MQTT messages to coordinate movements, avoid collisions, and reduce traffic incidents.

MQTT's support for Quality of Service (QoS) levels is particularly valuable in transportation, where message delivery guarantees can directly impact safety and reliability. For non-critical telemetry such as fuel level reporting, QoS 0 may suffice. However, for time-sensitive data like collision alerts or brake system faults, QoS 1 or QoS 2 ensures that these messages are reliably delivered and acknowledged by all intended recipients. MQTT's retained message feature also helps maintain the latest known status of critical parameters, such as the last reported position of a bus or the most recent signal status at an intersection.

Security is a key concern in automotive and transportation systems, given the potential consequences of compromised vehicle data or control channels. MQTT supports encrypted communication through Transport Layer Security (TLS), safeguarding data transmitted between vehicles, edge gateways, and backend servers. Additionally, MQTT brokers in transportation networks enforce authentication mechanisms and topic-level access controls to prevent unauthorized devices from injecting false data or hijacking control messages. This is especially important in scenarios where vehicles interact with critical infrastructure components like traffic management systems or toll collection units.

The integration of edge computing with MQTT is also accelerating within the transportation sector. Edge gateways located in vehicles or roadside units process data locally to reduce latency and minimize bandwidth usage. MQTT brokers deployed at the edge can manage communication between nearby devices, aggregating and filtering data before forwarding key insights to cloud platforms. This architecture supports faster decision-making for applications like predictive maintenance, driver assistance systems, and real-time traffic control, where milliseconds can make a significant difference in outcomes.

With the rise of electric vehicles (EVs), MQTT is playing an important role in the development of smart charging infrastructure. EV charging stations equipped with MQTT clients can publish data such as charging status, availability, power consumption, and fault reports to network operators. This enables EV owners to locate available charging stations in real-time and allows service providers to manage loads across the grid, optimize energy distribution, and schedule maintenance.

As the automotive and transportation industries continue to evolve toward greater automation, electrification, and connectivity, MQTT remains a fundamental enabler of this transformation. Its lightweight design, support for mobile environments, and compatibility with cloud and edge computing make it an indispensable tool for building scalable, efficient, and secure connected transportation systems. From connected cars and autonomous vehicles to logistics networks and public transit systems, MQTT helps bridge the gap between devices and data-driven services, driving innovation and improving outcomes across the mobility landscape.

MQTT and Healthcare IoT Solutions

The integration of IoT technologies into the healthcare sector has led to a new era of patient care, diagnostics, and operational efficiency. MQTT has emerged as a vital communication protocol in healthcare IoT solutions due to its lightweight nature, reliability, and real-time data exchange capabilities. In hospitals, clinics, and even home healthcare settings, a growing ecosystem of connected medical devices now leverages MQTT to deliver critical data to healthcare providers, ensuring that medical decisions are informed, timely, and accurate. The ability of MQTT to operate efficiently on resource-constrained devices and over limited or unreliable networks makes it ideal for diverse healthcare environments, from advanced urban hospitals to rural telehealth services.

One of the primary applications of MQTT in healthcare is in the realm of patient monitoring. Modern healthcare facilities deploy a wide range of monitoring equipment, such as heart rate monitors, blood pressure sensors, glucose meters, oxygen saturation devices, and electrocardiogram (ECG) machines. These devices continuously gather vital signs and patient metrics that need to be relayed to healthcare staff in real time. By integrating MQTT, medical devices can publish patient data to centralized brokers where hospital information systems, clinician dashboards, or mobile apps subscribed to specific patient topics can immediately access and display the information. For example, a heart rate monitor may publish to the topic hospital/room3/patient456/heart_rate, enabling nurses and physicians to receive instant updates and act on any abnormalities.

Remote patient monitoring, a growing trend in the healthcare industry, also benefits from MQTT's efficient design. In telemedicine and home healthcare scenarios, patients are often equipped with wearable devices that track their health metrics and send updates to healthcare providers. These devices frequently operate on constrained networks such as cellular or Wi-Fi connections with limited bandwidth. MQTT's minimal packet size and low overhead ensure that vital data is transmitted reliably without taxing the available network resources. This is especially critical in rural areas or underserved regions, where connectivity may be less stable. Patients suffering from chronic conditions like diabetes, hypertension, or respiratory illnesses can be continuously monitored outside clinical settings, reducing the need for frequent hospital visits and enabling early detection of potential complications.

The publish-subscribe model of MQTT also helps facilitate healthcare workflows by supporting event-driven communication. When an abnormal reading is detected, such as an irregular heartbeat or a dangerous drop in oxygen levels, the monitoring device can immediately publish an alert to a designated topic. The hospital's alert management system, subscribed to that topic, can then trigger notifications to attending medical staff or activate automated responses, such as adjusting ventilator settings. This event-driven model reduces latency in critical scenarios where every second counts, improving patient outcomes through faster intervention.

In addition to patient monitoring, MQTT is used to interconnect and coordinate various medical devices and systems within healthcare facilities. Hospital beds, infusion pumps, ventilators, and other medical equipment can integrate MQTT clients to report operational status, maintenance needs, or error codes. A centralized monitoring platform can subscribe to equipment-related topics and alert biomedical engineering teams when a device requires servicing or calibration. This proactive maintenance approach minimizes equipment downtime, reduces repair costs, and ensures that life-saving devices are always operational when needed.

The healthcare sector also deals with sensitive and regulated data, making security a paramount concern. MQTT addresses this by supporting Transport Layer Security (TLS) to encrypt data transmitted between devices and brokers. Healthcare providers often enforce additional security measures such as mutual TLS (mTLS) for device authentication, ensuring that only authorized medical devices can connect to the messaging system. Furthermore, MQTT brokers can implement topic-level access controls to limit data visibility to only those personnel or systems with the proper credentials. For example, a nurse's station dashboard might only have access to patient data from its assigned ward, while the hospital's central monitoring system may have broader visibility across multiple units.

Another crucial aspect of MQTT in healthcare IoT solutions is its compatibility with both edge and cloud computing. In critical care units or operating rooms, MQTT brokers may be deployed locally at the edge to ensure ultra-low latency communication between monitoring devices and decision-making systems. This guarantees that even if external internet connectivity is lost, local MQTT communications can continue to function, ensuring continuous patient monitoring. Data from these edge brokers can then be selectively forwarded to cloud platforms for long-term storage, analytics, and integration with electronic health records (EHR) systems.

Cloud-based MQTT deployments also facilitate advanced healthcare applications such as predictive analytics, AI-powered diagnostics, and machine learning models. Historical patient data transmitted via MQTT can be analyzed to identify patterns or predict medical events before they occur. For instance, machine learning algorithms trained on real-time and historical patient vitals may forecast the likelihood of sepsis or cardiac arrest, prompting early intervention and potentially saving lives. These insights are especially valuable in intensive care units (ICUs) or emergency departments, where conditions can deteriorate rapidly and require swift clinical action.

MQTT also plays a key role in telehealth consultations and remote diagnostics. Devices such as digital stethoscopes, connected ultrasound machines, and video conferencing systems use MQTT to share patient data, device status, and session metadata in real time with remote physicians. This enables healthcare providers to perform virtual assessments and diagnostics without the patient needing to travel, improving access to medical services for individuals in remote or isolated communities.

In addition, MQTT contributes to healthcare facility automation. Environmental sensors that monitor factors such as room temperature, humidity, air quality, and occupancy status can publish data over MQTT to building management systems. In hospital settings, where sterile environments and patient comfort are crucial, automation based on real-time sensor data helps maintain optimal conditions. For example, an HVAC system might adjust ventilation automatically in response to changes in air quality detected in an operating room.

The retained message feature of MQTT further enhances operational continuity in healthcare. When a new device, such as a clinician's tablet or nurse's station terminal, subscribes to a patient's topic, it can immediately retrieve the last known vital signs or alerts without waiting for a fresh data publication. This ensures that medical staff always have immediate access to the most up-to-date patient information, even when transitioning between devices or locations.

As the healthcare industry continues its digital transformation, MQTT has become a foundational technology enabling efficient, secure, and responsive healthcare IoT solutions. Its ability to support diverse communication scenarios, from bedside monitoring to cloud-based analytics, makes it a versatile tool for improving patient care, optimizing clinical workflows, and advancing healthcare innovation globally. Whether supporting in-hospital critical care, enhancing telehealth capabilities, or enabling remote patient monitoring, MQTT is shaping the future of connected healthcare systems.

MQTT and Agriculture: Smart Farming

The agriculture industry has witnessed a significant shift with the rise of smart farming, where traditional farming methods are augmented by connected technologies to enhance productivity, efficiency, and sustainability. At the heart of many smart farming solutions is MQTT, a lightweight messaging protocol well-suited for the demanding conditions and resource constraints often encountered in agricultural settings. By enabling real-time communication between sensors, machines, and cloud platforms, MQTT is helping farmers optimize crop yields, reduce operational costs, and make data-driven decisions across a range of agricultural applications.

Smart farming systems often rely on a variety of interconnected devices, including soil moisture sensors, weather stations, irrigation controllers, livestock monitors, and autonomous agricultural machinery. These devices must work together, often across vast and remote areas with limited network connectivity. MQTT's low-bandwidth and efficient communication model allows these devices to transmit data reliably over cellular, LPWAN, or satellite networks, which are frequently the only available options in rural environments. A soil moisture sensor located in a distant field, for example, may use MQTT to publish readings to a broker, which then delivers the data to an irrigation management system or a farmer's dashboard in near real time.

One of the fundamental applications of MQTT in agriculture is precision farming. Precision farming focuses on monitoring and managing the variability of soil and crop conditions across different zones of a farm. Sensors distributed across the field collect data on factors such as soil moisture, pH levels, nutrient concentrations, and temperature. These sensors publish telemetry data to MQTT topics such as farm1/fieldA/soil_moisture or farm1/fieldB/temperature. Decision-making platforms or control systems subscribe to these topics to adjust irrigation schedules, fertilizer application, and planting patterns. By ensuring that each section of the farm receives the optimal amount of water and nutrients, precision farming reduces resource waste and maximizes crop yields.

MQTT also plays a vital role in automating irrigation systems. Water scarcity and the need for efficient resource management have driven the adoption of smart irrigation solutions that rely on real-time data and automation to deliver water where and when it is needed most. MQTT enables moisture sensors and weather stations to trigger irrigation controllers based on dynamic field conditions. For instance, when a sensor detects low moisture levels in a specific section of a vineyard, it publishes a message to a topic that an irrigation controller subscribes to, automatically activating the drip irrigation system for that area. By integrating MQTT into this process, farmers can ensure precise and timely water delivery while minimizing labor costs and reducing water consumption.

In addition to crop management, MQTT is increasingly used in livestock farming to monitor animal health, behavior, and environmental conditions. Wearable devices attached to cattle or other livestock collect biometric data such as body temperature, heart rate, activity levels, and location. These devices publish data to MQTT topics like farm1/livestock/cow12/health. Farm management systems subscribe to these topics to detect early signs of illness, stress, or abnormal behavior. In the event that a cow exhibits signs of distress or deviates from its usual grazing patterns, automated alerts are sent to farmers, enabling early intervention and improving animal welfare.

Weather monitoring is another critical component of smart farming that benefits from MQTT integration. Agricultural operations are highly sensitive to weather conditions, including temperature, humidity, wind speed, and rainfall. Weather stations equipped with MQTT clients continuously publish local weather data, allowing farmers to make informed decisions about planting schedules, pesticide application, and harvest timing. By subscribing to weather-related topics such as farm1/weather/stationA/rainfall, farmers can receive real-time updates and forecasts directly to their control systems or mobile devices, reducing risks associated with adverse weather events.

The scalability of MQTT allows it to support both small farms with a handful of sensors and large agricultural enterprises managing thousands of devices across multiple locations. The protocol's ability to operate using hierarchical topic structures simplifies the organization of messages and devices within the system. A farm could organize its MQTT topics by dividing the property into fields, greenhouses, and livestock areas, enabling granular control and targeted automation across diverse agricultural zones. For instance, farm1/greenhouse1/humidity could be dedicated to monitoring the climate conditions within a greenhouse, while farm1/fieldC/fertilizer_dispenser would manage soil treatment operations in an open field.

Another valuable feature of MQTT in agricultural environments is its retained message functionality, which ensures that new subscribers immediately receive the most recent message published to a topic. In a remote farming operation, an irrigation management application could subscribe to an MQTT topic and instantly retrieve the latest soil moisture reading without waiting for the next sensor update. This is particularly useful when systems reboot, reconnect, or experience intermittent network availability due to rural connectivity challenges.

MQTT is also essential in supporting autonomous and semi-autonomous machinery used in modern farming operations. Tractors, harvesters, and drones equipped with GPS modules and telematics units use MQTT to relay their location, operational status, and sensor data to fleet management platforms. These platforms monitor machinery in real time and optimize their operation through automated task assignment and routing. For example, a self-driving tractor may publish its route progress and fuel level to farm1/machinery/tractor5/status, allowing farm managers to coordinate tasks remotely and ensure that field operations are completed efficiently.

The use of MQTT in agriculture extends beyond fieldwork and into supply chain and post-harvest logistics. Temperature-controlled storage facilities and transportation units, such as refrigerated trucks, rely on MQTT-enabled sensors to report temperature, humidity, and spoilage risks during the transportation of produce. This real-time visibility helps producers and distributors maintain product quality and reduce food waste by addressing issues before they impact the supply chain.

Security and data integrity are key concerns in smart farming, especially as farms adopt cloud-based solutions for data storage and remote management. MQTT supports secure communication through TLS encryption, preventing unauthorized access to sensitive operational data. Additionally, brokers can implement client authentication and access control policies to ensure that only trusted devices and users can interact with specific topics. This is essential when managing agricultural systems remotely, where data privacy and the reliability of automation systems must be preserved.

By enabling fast, reliable, and resource-efficient communication, MQTT has become an essential part of the smart farming revolution. It empowers farmers to automate routine tasks, optimize resource usage, improve animal and crop health, and respond rapidly to changing conditions in the field. As agriculture continues to evolve towards more sustainable and data-driven practices, MQTT will remain at the core of innovative solutions that enhance productivity while promoting environmental stewardship.

MQTT and Edge Computing

The convergence of MQTT and edge computing is shaping the next generation of IoT solutions by bringing processing power closer to where data is generated. Edge computing, as an architectural approach, decentralizes computation and storage from cloud or centralized data centers to devices or gateways located near the data sources. MQTT, with its lightweight and efficient messaging model, is naturally aligned with the requirements of edge computing, facilitating real-time communication between edge devices, local services, and centralized platforms. By leveraging MQTT at the edge, organizations are achieving faster response times, reducing bandwidth usage, and increasing system resilience.

Edge computing addresses several limitations found in cloud-centric IoT models. In many IoT deployments, especially in industrial environments, smart cities, or remote locations, relying solely on cloud processing introduces latency, increases dependency on internet connectivity, and can overload networks with massive amounts of raw data. MQTT's publish-subscribe model allows edge devices to communicate efficiently within local networks by utilizing an edge-deployed MQTT broker. This architecture enables local devices to publish sensor data, control messages, and alerts to the broker, while nearby applications or services subscribe to relevant topics to process information in real time.

Deploying MQTT brokers at the edge is a common practice in manufacturing plants, energy grids, and transportation systems. In a factory setting, edge brokers enable machinery, PLCs, and production line sensors to share data locally, ensuring that control decisions are made quickly and without reliance on cloud round-trips. For instance, a temperature sensor on a conveyor belt may publish readings to the topic factory1/line2/sensor5/temperature. An edge application subscribed to this topic can immediately process the data to regulate cooling fans or trigger alarms if overheating occurs. The local MQTT broker facilitates this interaction, ensuring low latency and continuous operation even if the external internet connection is disrupted.

One of the major benefits of combining MQTT with edge computing is network efficiency. IoT devices deployed in large-scale environments such as oil rigs, smart farms, or industrial plants generate significant volumes of telemetry data. Sending all of this data directly to the cloud would place strain on available bandwidth, increase cloud processing costs, and introduce unnecessary latency. Edge computing allows MQTT brokers and edge nodes to aggregate, filter, and preprocess data locally. Only essential or summarized information is then transmitted upstream to cloud platforms. For example, instead of continuously streaming every individual sensor reading, an edge service may publish aggregated metrics or anomaly alerts to cloud-based MQTT brokers, drastically reducing data transfer volumes.

The reliability and resilience of IoT systems are also improved when MQTT operates at the edge. In remote locations or mobile environments, such as maritime vessels, mining operations, or transportation fleets, network outages are common. Edge MQTT brokers allow local IoT networks to continue operating autonomously even when connectivity to the cloud is lost. Data can be buffered at the edge and forwarded once the connection is restored, while automation tasks such as triggering actuators or local machine learning inference continue without interruption. This ensures that mission-critical operations are not dependent on constant internet availability.

MQTT also enhances edge-to-cloud integration through its flexible topic structure and interoperability with various messaging and data processing tools. Edge brokers can bridge to cloud-based brokers, selectively forwarding messages while maintaining full control over what data leaves the local environment. This is particularly important in industries with regulatory or privacy constraints, where sensitive data must remain on-premises while non-sensitive information is shared with centralized platforms for analytics or storage. The bridging capability of MQTT ensures seamless communication between edge networks and cloud infrastructures without sacrificing data governance policies.

Security is a critical consideration when implementing MQTT in edge computing environments. Edge brokers act as a local security boundary, managing authentication and authorization for connected devices. Transport Layer Security (TLS) can be used to encrypt messages between devices and the edge broker, and between the edge broker and cloud services. Furthermore, brokers enforce access control lists (ACLs) to restrict which devices can publish or subscribe to specific topics, protecting sensitive operations and data from unauthorized access.

Edge computing powered by MQTT is also central to the rise of intelligent IoT systems. The processing capacity of edge nodes allows for the deployment of machine learning models, advanced rule engines, and event processing frameworks directly at the edge. MQTT acts as the messaging layer that feeds these services with real-time data streams. For instance, a predictive maintenance model running on an edge node might subscribe to vibration and temperature data from industrial equipment, analyzing patterns to forecast potential failures. If an anomaly is detected, the model can immediately publish a warning to a local topic, prompting human operators or automated systems to take corrective action.

Smart city applications are another domain where MQTT and edge computing are frequently paired. In traffic management systems, edge brokers deployed at intersections or roadside units collect and distribute data from traffic cameras, vehicle counters, and environmental sensors. This allows for real-time adjustments to traffic light timing, electronic signage updates, and emergency vehicle prioritization without relying on a central cloud server. The decentralized approach improves system responsiveness and reduces congestion in urban networks.

MQTT also contributes to the scalability of edge computing solutions. As new sensors, machines, or subsystems are added to an existing network, they can quickly integrate by publishing to or subscribing from the local MQTT broker. The broker's publish-subscribe model eliminates the need for complex direct integrations between devices, promoting modular system design and simplifying deployment and maintenance. Whether adding a new production line sensor, installing a weather station on a smart farm, or deploying a new surveillance camera in a city, MQTT at the edge allows devices to become part of the network with minimal configuration.

Another advantage is the flexibility provided by MQTT's support for retained messages and persistent sessions. Devices that temporarily disconnect due to power cycles or network fluctuations can resume communication without losing critical data. Edge brokers retain essential system status messages, such as last known configurations or alert conditions, ensuring that newly connected or restarted devices immediately receive up-to-date context.

As edge computing continues to grow in relevance, especially in industries requiring fast decision-making and reduced cloud dependency, MQTT has proven to be an essential enabler of this evolution. It provides the robust, lightweight, and flexible communication layer needed to support distributed, autonomous systems operating at the network edge. By facilitating efficient data exchange, enabling rapid local processing, and maintaining connectivity to cloud platforms, MQTT is shaping the future of scalable and intelligent edge computing architectures across a wide range of industries.

MQTT and 5G Networks

The combination of MQTT and 5G networks is redefining the possibilities for IoT deployments, unlocking new levels of speed, reliability, and scalability across a range of industries. While MQTT has long been valued for its efficiency and low-bandwidth requirements, the advent of 5G provides an ideal environment for the protocol to flourish in even more demanding use cases. Together, MQTT and 5G enable highly responsive, real-time communication between devices and platforms, making them the backbone of next-generation applications in smart cities, autonomous vehicles, industrial automation, healthcare, and beyond.

5G networks offer ultra-low latency, massive device connectivity, and significantly higher data transfer rates compared to previous mobile network generations. These capabilities align perfectly with MQTT's lightweight publish-subscribe model, which is designed to reduce overhead while facilitating asynchronous message exchange. In dense urban areas or sprawling industrial campuses, thousands or even millions of MQTT-enabled IoT devices can simultaneously connect over 5G infrastructure without overwhelming the network. MQTT brokers deployed on edge servers or within cloud regions can seamlessly handle this influx of data, enabling large-scale IoT ecosystems to operate smoothly.

One of the most significant advantages of using MQTT over 5G is the ability to support latency-sensitive applications. With 5G's promise of end-to-end latencies as low as one millisecond, MQTT-based systems can now meet the stringent real-time requirements of advanced use cases. For example, autonomous vehicles rely on near-instantaneous communication between onboard sensors, edge computing nodes, and centralized systems. MQTT over 5G allows for rapid transmission of sensor data, such as object detection or vehicle telemetry, to remote control centers or other vehicles. The reduced latency ensures timely decision-making for critical tasks like collision avoidance, adaptive cruise control, or autonomous navigation in dynamic traffic conditions.

In industrial automation, 5G combined with MQTT is enabling factories to deploy wireless sensors, actuators, and robotic systems at scale. The high reliability and ultra-low latency of 5G allow industrial devices to function without the constraints of wired networks. MQTT's lightweight footprint ensures that machine controllers, PLCs, and production line sensors can publish and subscribe to topics with minimal delay, coordinating assembly lines and manufacturing processes in real time. This wireless flexibility fosters new levels of agility in production environments, where rapid reconfiguration and mobile machinery are becoming increasingly common.

Smart cities are another domain benefiting from the synergy between MQTT and 5G. Urban infrastructure, including traffic management systems, street lighting, waste collection, and environmental monitoring, requires reliable, wide-area communication between a vast number of distributed devices. 5G networks can handle the high density of connections while ensuring that MQTT-powered devices communicate efficiently. For instance, traffic cameras may publish congestion data to city/traffic/intersection7/flow, which is then used by adaptive traffic control systems to adjust signal timings on the fly. Air quality sensors located throughout the city publish real-time pollution data to city/environment/zone3/air_quality, which is consumed by public health platforms and alerting systems.

In healthcare, 5G and MQTT are driving the next wave of connected medical devices and remote patient monitoring systems. Wearable devices, such as heart monitors and glucose sensors, benefit from the expansive coverage and reduced latency of 5G, allowing patients to transmit critical health data to care providers in real time. MQTT's ability to minimize network overhead ensures that these wearable devices can operate efficiently on mobile networks, extending battery life and reducing costs. In emergency scenarios, ambulances equipped with 5G connectivity and MQTT clients can continuously stream vital patient information to hospitals, enabling medical teams to prepare in advance for patient arrival.

Another key area where MQTT and 5G work synergistically is in augmented reality (AR) and virtual reality (VR) applications, which are increasingly used in fields such as remote maintenance, training, and logistics. AR headsets and VR devices demand both high data throughput and minimal latency to ensure a seamless user experience. MQTT, when integrated with 5G-enabled edge computing nodes, can deliver real-time data streams to these devices, supporting immersive and interactive environments. For instance, technicians performing equipment maintenance may receive live sensor data and procedural instructions via AR glasses, all synchronized through MQTT messages transmitted over 5G networks.

The scalability provided by 5G networks is also instrumental in expanding MQTT deployments into areas where massive IoT networks are required. Agricultural applications, such as precision farming, involve deploying large numbers of distributed sensors across wide rural areas. With 5G's support for massive machine-type communication (mMTC), farmers can implement dense sensor grids to monitor soil conditions, crop health, and weather patterns. MQTT ensures that these sensors transmit data efficiently, supporting automated irrigation, fertilization, and pest management strategies with real-time intelligence gathered directly from the field.

Security is another area where MQTT and 5G complement each other. MQTT brokers leverage TLS encryption and robust authentication mechanisms to protect data exchanges, while 5G networks add another layer of security through network slicing and improved encryption at the radio and core network levels. Network slicing allows operators to allocate dedicated virtual network resources to specific applications or organizations, ensuring that MQTT traffic for critical systems, such as public safety or industrial automation, operates on isolated and highly secure segments of the 5G network.

Edge computing, when integrated with MQTT and 5G, takes these benefits even further. By deploying MQTT brokers and edge nodes within 5G network infrastructure, such as at base stations or micro data centers, organizations can process data closer to the source. This minimizes round-trip times to the cloud and enables ultra-responsive applications that require immediate local decision-making. For instance, in autonomous drone operations, MQTT brokers running on edge nodes within the 5G network can coordinate flight paths, obstacle detection, and swarm intelligence among drones without depending on distant cloud platforms.

The mobility support of 5G is particularly beneficial for MQTT clients embedded in mobile devices, vehicles, and machinery. As these devices move between different geographic areas, 5G ensures seamless handover between network cells, maintaining uninterrupted MQTT connections with brokers. This is essential in logistics and fleet management, where vehicles constantly change locations but must continuously report telemetry data, delivery statuses, or environmental conditions. MQTT over 5G enables these mobile assets to remain connected to operational platforms, providing real-time visibility and allowing for dynamic adjustments to routes or schedules.

The synergy between MQTT and 5G is also evident in the realm of content delivery and multimedia streaming. Digital signage networks in smart cities and retail environments can leverage MQTT over 5G to distribute content updates, advertising campaigns, and system status messages to thousands of screens simultaneously. By combining MQTT's efficient messaging system with the high data rates of 5G, these networks can deliver rich media content while maintaining low operational costs and reducing latency.

Ultimately, the combination of MQTT and 5G creates a robust foundation for building distributed, responsive, and highly scalable IoT systems. Together, they enable organizations to harness real-time data streams, automate complex processes, and deliver intelligent services across industries and geographies. As 5G networks continue to roll out globally, the role of MQTT as a lightweight and versatile messaging protocol will only become more central to unlocking the full potential of this next-generation connectivity revolution.

Comparing MQTT with HTTP, CoAP, and AMQP

When designing IoT and distributed systems, choosing the right messaging protocol is a crucial decision that influences system efficiency, scalability, and responsiveness. MQTT is often selected for its lightweight design and efficient publish-subscribe architecture, but it is not the only protocol available. HTTP, CoAP, and AMQP are also widely used in IoT and M2M (machine-to-machine) communication scenarios, each offering different strengths and trade-offs. By comparing these protocols, we can better understand where MQTT stands out and where other protocols might be more appropriate depending on the application context.

MQTT was created specifically for low-bandwidth, high-latency, and unreliable network environments, making it an ideal protocol for IoT devices and embedded systems. Its design centers on a broker-based publish-subscribe model where devices send messages to a central broker, which then routes them to subscribers based on topic filters.

This decoupling of publishers and subscribers increases system flexibility and scalability, allowing devices to exchange messages asynchronously without requiring knowledge of one another's network details. MQTT's minimal packet overhead and low power consumption make it highly suitable for resource-constrained devices operating on cellular networks or in remote locations where bandwidth is limited.

HTTP, on the other hand, is the dominant protocol of the internet and is widely used for web-based applications and RESTful APIs. Unlike MQTT, HTTP follows a request-response model where a client sends a request to a server and waits for a response. This synchronous communication model is straightforward but can introduce latency and inefficiencies in IoT applications where devices must frequently transmit small data packets or respond to real-time events. HTTP headers are also significantly larger than MQTT's minimal headers, resulting in higher bandwidth consumption, which may strain networks in sensor-heavy environments or battery-powered devices. However, HTTP benefits from broad support across programming languages, tools, and infrastructure, making it a suitable choice for non-time-sensitive applications, configuration services, or scenarios where human-machine interaction, such as user dashboards, is prioritized over machine-to-machine data exchange.

CoAP, the Constrained Application Protocol, is another protocol tailored to IoT and embedded systems, designed by the IETF for use over constrained networks and devices. Like HTTP, CoAP follows a request-response model but is optimized for low-power and low-bandwidth environments. CoAP operates over UDP rather than TCP, reducing the overhead associated with connection-oriented protocols and enabling faster message delivery in lossy networks. CoAP's use of a compact binary header and its support for multicast communication make it efficient for group messaging in sensor networks. Additionally, CoAP integrates natively with web technologies by providing a RESTful interface that mirrors HTTP methods such as GET, POST, PUT, and DELETE. However, CoAP lacks the native broker-based publish-subscribe model found in MQTT and typically requires additional middleware if pub-sub functionality is needed. This makes MQTT a more natural choice in scenarios where asynchronous event distribution and decoupled communication between devices are required.

AMQP, or the Advanced Message Queuing Protocol, is designed for enterprise-grade messaging systems and supports a wide range of communication patterns, including publish-subscribe, point-to-point, and request-response. Unlike MQTT's simplicity, AMQP is a feature-rich protocol that includes built-in support for transactions, message queues, topic exchanges, message acknowledgments, and security policies. AMQP is often favored in financial services, supply chain management, and other business-critical applications that require guaranteed message delivery, routing flexibility, and extensive security controls. However, AMQP's complexity and overhead make it less suitable for constrained IoT devices. AMQP messages have larger headers, and the protocol itself demands more resources in terms of memory and processing power, making it better suited for backend systems, data centers, and cloud applications rather than low-power edge devices.

While MQTT prioritizes minimalism and simplicity, AMQP is designed for robustness and configurability in high-throughput and transactional environments. Both protocols support Quality of Service (QoS) levels, but MQTT focuses on providing lightweight QoS 0, 1, and 2 for reliability without sacrificing efficiency. In contrast, AMQP offers more granular delivery controls, such as message transactions and acknowledgment mechanisms tailored to complex business workflows.

One of the distinctive features of MQTT compared to HTTP and CoAP is its persistent session and retained message capabilities. MQTT clients can establish persistent sessions with the broker, enabling them to receive queued messages even after reconnecting from an offline state. Retained messages allow the broker to store the last known message on a topic and deliver it to new subscribers upon connection. Neither HTTP nor CoAP provides these features natively, often requiring additional software layers or custom implementation to achieve similar functionality.

In terms of security, all four protocols support encryption, though implementation varies depending on the protocol stack. MQTT relies on TLS to encrypt data during transit, while HTTP uses HTTPS, and CoAP supports Datagram Transport Layer Security (DTLS) due to its use of UDP. AMQP typically operates over TLS as well but offers more integrated authentication and authorization features within its specification. Security considerations often depend more on the deployment context, such as the use of network-level protections, access control policies, and secure broker or server configurations.

Scalability is another critical factor in protocol selection. MQTT is particularly well-suited for scaling large IoT deployments due to its publish-subscribe model and efficient bandwidth usage. A single MQTT broker can handle thousands of concurrent client connections and millions of topic-based messages with relatively modest hardware requirements. HTTP servers can also scale effectively, especially when integrated with load balancers and caching layers, but the overhead associated with HTTP headers and repeated connection setups makes it less efficient for many-to-many IoT messaging scenarios. CoAP excels in smaller, local networks where rapid request-response exchanges are sufficient, while AMQP's scalability is oriented toward complex, large-scale enterprise systems where message reliability and transactional integrity are paramount.

Overall, MQTT's design makes it ideal for IoT environments where devices need to communicate asynchronously, operate on constrained hardware, and conserve bandwidth. HTTP remains the go-to protocol for web-facing services and APIs, where human interaction and request-response patterns dominate. CoAP serves well in constrained networks with a preference for RESTful interaction models and multicast support. AMQP, with its rich feature set and reliability guarantees, is best suited for enterprise environments demanding sophisticated messaging capabilities. Selecting the right protocol ultimately depends on the specific needs of the application, device limitations, and network conditions, with MQTT offering a compelling balance of simplicity, efficiency, and reliability for a wide array of IoT and M2M communication scenarios.

MQTT-SN: MQTT for Sensor Networks

MQTT-SN, which stands for MQTT for Sensor Networks, is a specialized version of the MQTT protocol designed specifically to address the limitations and requirements of wireless sensor networks (WSNs) and other highly constrained environments. While traditional

MQTT is already lightweight and well-suited for low-power devices, it relies on the TCP transport layer, which can be inefficient and resource-intensive for sensor nodes that operate with severe power, memory, and bandwidth constraints. MQTT-SN introduces optimizations and protocol modifications that enable seamless communication between sensor networks and standard MQTT brokers while significantly reducing communication overhead.

The primary difference between MQTT and MQTT-SN lies in the transport layer. MQTT-SN is designed to operate over connectionless and lightweight transport protocols, typically User Datagram Protocol (UDP) or other data link layer protocols commonly used in wireless sensor networks, such as Zigbee or Bluetooth Low Energy (BLE). By eliminating the overhead of TCP's connection-oriented features, MQTT-SN reduces the energy consumption and memory footprint required by constrained sensor nodes, making it better suited for battery-powered devices and large-scale sensor deployments in remote or infrastructure-limited areas.

MQTT-SN preserves the core publish-subscribe communication model of MQTT, ensuring compatibility with existing MQTT ecosystems. Sensor nodes running MQTT-SN can publish data to topics, subscribe to topics of interest, and receive messages through the broker. However, MQTT-SN introduces a new layer called the MQTT-SN Gateway, which acts as an intermediary between MQTT-SN clients (sensors) and standard MQTT brokers. The gateway is responsible for translating MQTT-SN messages into standard MQTT format and vice versa. This ensures interoperability between lightweight sensor networks and cloud-based or enterprise MQTT infrastructures, allowing data from the edge to be easily integrated into larger IoT platforms.

To further optimize communication, MQTT-SN introduces topic name aliases. In standard MQTT, topic names are often long strings that describe the hierarchy and structure of the system, such as factory1/lineA/sensor5/temperature. While this is efficient on traditional IP networks, transmitting lengthy topic strings over low-power wireless networks can quickly consume valuable bandwidth and energy. MQTT-SN addresses this by using short, numeric topic identifiers instead of full topic strings. These topic IDs are pre-registered with the MQTT-SN gateway during the initialization phase, enabling subsequent messages to reference topics using compact numerical values rather than full strings, greatly reducing message size.

Another enhancement introduced by MQTT-SN is its support for sleeping clients, a crucial feature for battery-powered sensors that need to conserve energy. Many sensor nodes operate in duty-cycled modes, where they spend most of their time in low-power sleep states and only wake up periodically to transmit or receive data. MQTT-SN's protocol accommodates this by allowing sleeping clients to inform the gateway of their sleep schedules. The gateway can then buffer incoming messages intended for sleeping clients and deliver them once the client wakes up and reestablishes communication. This ensures that no critical messages are lost while maintaining the device's energy efficiency.

MQTT-SN also modifies how sessions are managed. While traditional MQTT uses TCP-based persistent sessions, MQTT-SN supports lightweight session management suitable for the intermittent nature of sensor networks. Clients can indicate whether they require session persistence during the connection process, allowing the gateway to store session information, such as topic subscriptions, while the client is offline. This reduces the overhead involved in resubscribing to topics each time a sensor wakes up, streamlining communication and conserving additional energy.

Security in MQTT-SN implementations is often achieved by combining network-layer encryption with lightweight application-layer security. While MQTT-SN itself does not define a specific encryption mechanism, it is typically deployed over secure transport layers like DTLS when using UDP or leverages the security features of wireless technologies like Zigbee or BLE. Additionally, MQTT-SN gateways can enforce access control policies, client authentication, and topic-level permissions to protect the integrity and confidentiality of data as it flows from the sensor network to the MQTT broker and beyond.

The use cases for MQTT-SN span a wide range of industries. In agriculture, wireless sensor networks equipped with MQTT-SN clients monitor soil moisture, temperature, and nutrient levels across large farms. These sensors relay data to a nearby MQTT-SN gateway connected to an MQTT broker, enabling farmers to make informed irrigation and fertilization decisions while minimizing water and resource waste. In environmental monitoring, MQTT-SN sensors deployed in forests or mountainous regions track air quality, humidity, and wildlife activity, relaying insights to researchers or conservationists with minimal power consumption.

Smart buildings also benefit from MQTT-SN's efficiency. Networks of battery-powered occupancy sensors, light level detectors, and HVAC controllers communicate via MQTT-SN to a building management gateway, which then integrates this data into a broader MQTT-based system. By optimizing energy usage based on real-time occupancy and environmental data, facilities can significantly reduce operational costs and improve occupant comfort.

In industrial settings, MQTT-SN is used in scenarios where deploying wired connections is impractical or cost-prohibitive. Wireless sensor networks using MQTT-SN monitor machine vibration, temperature, and performance metrics to detect early signs of wear or failure. Maintenance teams receive timely alerts through the MQTT broker and can take preemptive action before costly breakdowns occur.

Overall, MQTT-SN serves as a specialized extension of the MQTT protocol, tailored to meet the unique requirements of wireless sensor networks and ultra-constrained IoT devices. Its ability to operate over lightweight transport layers, reduce message sizes through topic aliases, and support sleeping clients makes it an ideal solution for environments where power conservation, network efficiency, and scalability are paramount. By bridging the gap between low-power edge devices and full-scale MQTT ecosystems, MQTT-SN enables seamless data flow and fosters the creation of robust, responsive, and efficient IoT architectures across diverse industries and applications.

MQTT Brokers: Open Source vs. Commercial

When deploying an MQTT-based system, one of the most important architectural decisions is selecting the right MQTT broker. The broker acts as the central hub for all message exchanges, handling the distribution of data between publishers and subscribers. The market offers a wide range of MQTT brokers, categorized broadly into open-source and commercial solutions. Both options have distinct advantages and trade-offs, depending on the requirements of the project, including scalability, security, support, and budget.

Open-source MQTT brokers are widely adopted due to their flexibility, cost-effectiveness, and active community support. Popular open-source brokers such as Eclipse Mosquitto, EMQX Community Edition, VerneMQ, and HiveMQ Community Edition offer robust implementations of the MQTT protocol, with core features including publish-subscribe messaging, Quality of Service (QoS) levels, retained messages, and session persistence. These brokers are ideal for developers looking for a lightweight and customizable broker that can be deployed on various platforms, from embedded devices and edge gateways to virtual machines and cloud instances.

Eclipse Mosquitto, one of the most recognized open-source brokers, is praised for its simplicity and small footprint, making it well-suited for resource-constrained environments. Its easy installation process and wide compatibility with MQTT client libraries have made it a favorite among hobbyists, IoT startups, and academic projects. However, while Mosquitto performs admirably in small to medium-sized deployments, scaling to handle tens or hundreds of thousands of concurrent connections may require external tools like load balancers or clustering workarounds, which add complexity to the system architecture.

VerneMQ and EMQX Community Edition, both written in Erlang, are open-source brokers designed with scalability and fault tolerance in mind. These brokers support clustering out of the box, enabling developers to distribute workloads across multiple nodes and achieve higher availability. Clustering allows MQTT messages to be shared across broker nodes, providing resilience against node failures and allowing the system to handle large-scale deployments. Open-source brokers often attract organizations that value full control over their infrastructure and prefer to modify or extend the broker's functionality to meet unique operational needs.

Despite the appeal of open-source brokers, they typically come with limitations in terms of official support, advanced features, and enterprise-grade integrations. While community forums and open-source contributors can offer valuable troubleshooting assistance, organizations deploying MQTT in mission-critical applications may require service level agreements (SLAs), dedicated technical support, and advanced security features, which are often not guaranteed in open-source solutions.

This is where commercial MQTT brokers come into play. Companies such as HiveMQ, EMQ Technologies, and Solace offer commercial-grade MQTT brokers with extended feature sets, professional support, and robust performance optimizations. HiveMQ Enterprise, for example, provides an MQTT broker designed for large-scale and enterprise IoT deployments, supporting millions of concurrent connections, highly configurable clustering, and detailed monitoring capabilities through built-in dashboards and REST APIs. HiveMQ also offers integrations with enterprise systems, such as Kafka, databases, and analytics platforms, allowing organizations to streamline data pipelines and accelerate IoT project development.

Commercial brokers often include advanced security mechanisms out of the box. Features such as role-based access control (RBAC), OAuth2 integration, custom authentication and authorization plugins, and fine-grained topic-level permissions are typically standard in commercial solutions. This is particularly important for industries with strict regulatory compliance requirements, such as finance, healthcare, and critical infrastructure. For example, an energy company deploying an MQTT-based system to monitor a smart grid may prioritize the robust security, auditing capabilities, and 24/7 technical support offered by a commercial broker to meet operational and regulatory demands.

Performance optimization is another benefit associated with commercial MQTT brokers. Vendors invest in continuous performance tuning, ensuring their brokers are capable of handling high message throughput, minimal latency, and reliable delivery even under heavy load conditions. Some commercial brokers are optimized to operate across hybrid cloud and edge environments, supporting use cases where data processing must be distributed across geographically diverse locations while maintaining seamless communication between edge nodes and centralized cloud systems.

Scalability is addressed differently depending on the broker type. While open-source brokers such as EMQX and VerneMQ provide clustering capabilities, commercial offerings typically enhance these features with more sophisticated load balancing, dynamic scaling, and multi-tenant support. HiveMQ Enterprise, for instance, supports horizontal scaling with automatic discovery and load distribution between nodes, reducing the complexity of managing large clusters.

Commercial MQTT brokers also provide extensive monitoring and observability tools to help administrators gain insights into system health, message flows, client behavior, and performance bottlenecks. These capabilities are often integrated into centralized management platforms, offering visual dashboards, metrics export to third-party monitoring tools like Prometheus or Grafana, and automated alerts to detect anomalies. While similar functionality can be implemented on open-source brokers using additional tools or plugins, commercial brokers simplify these tasks with native integrations and dedicated support.

Cost is a significant factor when choosing between open-source and commercial MQTT brokers. Open-source brokers have no licensing fees, making them attractive to startups, small businesses, or proof-of-concept projects with limited budgets. However, the total cost of ownership for open-source solutions can increase when considering the resources needed for configuration, maintenance, security hardening, and scaling, especially in complex deployments.

Commercial brokers, while requiring licensing fees or subscription models, reduce operational burdens by providing comprehensive support, streamlined management, and enterprise-ready features. Organizations with time-sensitive projects or limited internal expertise may find the investment in a commercial broker justified by the accelerated deployment timeline, reduced risk of downtime, and professional guidance available throughout the project lifecycle.

Ultimately, the choice between open-source and commercial MQTT brokers depends on project scale, security requirements, available technical expertise, and long-term operational goals. Open-source solutions offer flexibility, community innovation, and cost-efficiency for smaller or less complex systems. Commercial brokers provide feature-rich, scalable, and secure platforms suitable for enterprises aiming to deploy large-scale, mission-critical IoT systems with full vendor support. By carefully weighing the trade-offs, organizations can select the broker solution that best aligns with their technical and business needs.

Load Balancing and High Availability

In MQTT-based systems, ensuring scalability, reliability, and uptime is crucial, especially when supporting large-scale IoT deployments or mission-critical applications. Load balancing and high availability are two key strategies employed to meet these demands. Both concepts aim to ensure that MQTT brokers can handle a growing number of client connections and message throughput while minimizing the risk of service disruptions due to failures or traffic spikes.

Load balancing refers to the process of distributing incoming MQTT client connections and message traffic across multiple brokers or nodes within a cluster. As the number of connected devices in an IoT network increases, a single broker may become a bottleneck, unable to efficiently handle the load. A load balancer positioned in front of the MQTT broker cluster helps manage this challenge by distributing client connections evenly across available broker instances. This prevents any single broker from being overwhelmed, ensuring optimal resource utilization and maintaining system performance.

There are different methods of implementing load balancing in MQTT architectures. One common approach involves using a Layer 4 load balancer, which operates at the transport layer and distributes traffic based on IP address and port. This method is simple, fast, and efficient for balancing TCP-based MQTT traffic. Alternatively, a Layer 7 load balancer, which operates at the application layer, can make more intelligent routing decisions based on protocol-specific information such as client identifiers or custom headers. While Layer 7 load balancing adds slightly more overhead, it provides greater flexibility in managing MQTT client sessions and routing traffic based on predefined policies.

In many deployments, especially cloud-based or hybrid environments, DNS-based load balancing is also employed. This approach distributes traffic by resolving a single domain name to multiple broker IP addresses, allowing clients to connect to the broker instance closest to them geographically. DNS load balancing can be combined with health checks to ensure that clients are only directed to healthy broker nodes. While simple to implement, DNS-based methods lack real-time traffic awareness and session persistence, which can lead to uneven distribution under certain conditions.

High availability (HA) complements load balancing by ensuring that the MQTT system remains operational in the event of broker node failures, network outages, or hardware issues. In an HA setup, multiple broker instances are configured in a cluster, where they replicate data, share session states, and synchronize topic subscriptions to ensure seamless failover. If one broker node fails, connected clients are automatically redirected to a healthy broker without data loss or service interruption.

Clustering is a common strategy used to achieve high availability in MQTT systems. In a clustered setup, broker nodes communicate with each other to replicate essential state information such as retained messages, client subscriptions, and QoS 1 or QoS 2 message queues. This synchronization ensures that clients reconnecting to a different node after a failure will resume operations without missing messages or needing to re-subscribe manually. Open-source brokers such as VerneMQ and EMQX, as well as commercial solutions like HiveMQ Enterprise, offer native clustering capabilities that facilitate high availability and fault tolerance.

A critical component of maintaining HA is session persistence. MQTT clients that use persistent sessions can reconnect to a different broker node in the cluster without losing the context of their previous session. This includes retaining information about topics the client was subscribed to and ensuring that any QoS 1 or QoS 2 messages pending delivery are still queued and forwarded once the connection is reestablished. Brokers that support distributed session persistence across the cluster make it easier to ensure uninterrupted client experience during node failures or maintenance events.

To further enhance resilience, MQTT deployments often incorporate geographic redundancy by deploying broker clusters across multiple data centers or cloud regions. In this architecture, each cluster operates independently but can synchronize data through inter-cluster replication mechanisms or through upstream systems such as data lakes or event streaming platforms. Geographic redundancy helps protect against regional outages, enabling business continuity for global IoT networks.

Health checks and automated failover mechanisms are essential for managing broker clusters effectively. Load balancers and cluster management tools continuously monitor the health of each broker instance, verifying availability through heartbeat signals, response times, or specific broker metrics. If a broker becomes unresponsive or experiences degraded performance, traffic is automatically rerouted to healthy nodes. Modern load balancers and orchestration platforms such as Kubernetes can integrate health monitoring and auto-scaling features, ensuring that additional broker instances are deployed dynamically to meet increased demand.

Load balancing and high availability also require attention to broker resource utilization, including CPU, memory, disk I/O, and network throughput. Brokers need sufficient resources to handle message routing, QoS guarantees, session persistence, and clustering overhead, particularly in large-scale IoT applications. Horizontal scaling, where new broker instances are added to the cluster to accommodate growth, is often preferred over vertical scaling, which focuses on increasing the capacity of individual broker nodes. Horizontal scaling provides more flexibility and resilience, reducing the risk of a single point of failure.

Security must also be considered when implementing load balancing and HA. TLS termination, client authentication, and access control policies need to be consistently enforced across all broker instances. Load balancers that terminate TLS connections must securely forward traffic to internal broker nodes or allow for end-to-end encryption if security policies require it. Additionally, cluster communication between broker nodes should be encrypted and authenticated to prevent unauthorized access to internal broker synchronization traffic.

Observability and monitoring tools play a critical role in maintaining effective load balancing and HA. Metrics related to connection counts, message throughput, dropped packets, broker uptime, and latency should be continuously collected and visualized through dashboards. Alerts should be configured to notify administrators of potential performance bottlenecks or node failures before they impact clients. Tools such as Prometheus, Grafana, and ELK (Elasticsearch, Logstash, Kibana) stacks are frequently integrated with MQTT broker clusters to provide real-time monitoring and log analysis.

Ultimately, load balancing and high availability are essential strategies for building resilient, scalable, and efficient MQTT systems. By distributing client connections, optimizing resource usage, and providing seamless failover, these techniques ensure that IoT applications remain responsive and reliable even under challenging conditions or high traffic loads. Whether powering connected vehicles, smart city infrastructure, industrial automation, or healthcare monitoring systems, MQTT broker clusters designed with load balancing and HA principles form the backbone of modern, large-scale IoT ecosystems.

Scaling MQTT Deployments

As IoT ecosystems grow and the number of connected devices rises into the thousands or even millions, scaling MQTT deployments becomes a critical architectural challenge. While MQTT is inherently designed to be lightweight and efficient, supporting small-scale networks with minimal resources, scaling it for enterprise-grade systems requires careful planning and execution. A scalable MQTT deployment must accommodate increasing numbers of clients, rising message throughput, and ensure consistent performance and reliability under diverse operational conditions.

The first step in scaling MQTT deployments is to understand the limitations of a single broker setup. A single MQTT broker running on a dedicated server or virtual machine may be sufficient for small networks, such as smart home systems or localized sensor networks. However, as the client base expands, the broker may struggle to handle the volume of concurrent connections and the surge in message traffic. CPU, memory, disk I/O, and network bandwidth can all become bottlenecks. Overloading a broker can result in dropped connections, increased message latency, and reduced Quality of Service (QoS) guarantees. Therefore, scaling starts by addressing both vertical and horizontal strategies.

Vertical scaling refers to increasing the capacity of the broker host by adding more CPU cores, memory, or network bandwidth to a single machine. While this can improve performance to a degree, vertical scaling has its limits. Hardware upgrades cannot continue indefinitely, and the failure of a single, overburdened broker becomes a single point of failure for the entire system. To overcome this, horizontal scaling is implemented by distributing the workload across multiple broker nodes, typically arranged in a clustered architecture.

Clustering is a widely adopted method to scale MQTT brokers horizontally. In a cluster, multiple broker nodes work together as a unified system, sharing client connections, topic subscriptions, retained messages, and session states. This allows incoming client connections to be distributed across nodes, balancing the load and preventing individual brokers from becoming overloaded. Each broker in the cluster communicates with its peers to synchronize session information and ensure high availability, meaning that clients can reconnect to any healthy node without service disruption in the event of a failure.

Effective clustering requires a load balancing mechanism to direct clients to different broker nodes. Load balancers, whether Layer 4 or Layer 7, sit in front of the broker cluster and distribute incoming TCP or WebSocket connections based on real-time metrics such as active connections, CPU utilization, or geographic proximity. Advanced load balancers may also support session persistence, which helps ensure that a client reconnects to the same broker node to take advantage of local session caches, reducing the need for additional synchronization traffic across the cluster.

Another key aspect of scaling MQTT deployments is optimizing broker configurations. Each broker instance should be tuned according to the expected workload. This involves setting limits on the maximum number of concurrent client connections, adjusting TCP backlog queues, tuning keep-alive intervals, and configuring QoS-related settings to balance reliability with system performance. For high-throughput scenarios, it is common to limit the use of QoS 2 messages, as they introduce additional acknowledgment traffic and processing overhead. Many large-scale deployments default to QoS 0 or QoS 1, depending on the criticality of message delivery.

Scaling MQTT also extends to storage systems. MQTT brokers that retain messages or support persistent sessions often rely on file systems, databases, or message queues to store session and message data. In large deployments, it is critical to choose high-performance storage backends and optimize them for low latency and high write throughput. Distributed storage systems such as Cassandra, Redis, or high-speed SSD arrays are often integrated with broker clusters to manage persistent data efficiently.

Network design plays a pivotal role in large-scale MQTT deployments. As message rates increase, brokers may generate significant traffic, especially in use cases such as connected vehicles or industrial automation. Deployments should consider network segmentation, separating broker-to-broker communication, client ingress traffic, and broker-to-application or broker-to-cloud traffic into dedicated subnets or VLANs. This reduces congestion, enhances security, and improves the overall stability of the system. In cloud-native environments, using Virtual Private Clouds (VPCs) or Kubernetes network policies further helps to isolate and manage traffic flows.

Scalability is also influenced by how MQTT brokers interact with downstream systems. As brokers scale to handle massive message ingestion from IoT devices, it is crucial to integrate them effectively with cloud platforms, analytics engines, and data lakes. Many brokers, especially commercial offerings, include built-in connectors to stream MQTT messages directly into platforms such as Apache Kafka, Amazon Kinesis, or Google Pub/Sub. These integrations help decouple data ingestion from processing, allowing backend systems to scale independently and handle the high-velocity data streams generated by millions of devices.

Another approach to scaling is through edge-to-cloud architectures. Edge brokers are deployed closer to devices, aggregating data locally before forwarding it to centralized cloud brokers. This reduces the number of connections handled by cloud brokers and minimizes bandwidth usage over wide-area networks. The edge brokers can also preprocess, filter, or batch messages, sending only critical or aggregated data upstream. This hierarchical broker model distributes workload more efficiently, enhancing both scalability and system resilience.

Monitoring and observability are indispensable when scaling MQTT systems. As broker clusters grow, administrators must continuously monitor metrics such as connection counts, message publish rates, queue lengths, CPU and memory utilization, and message latency. Deploying monitoring solutions like Prometheus and Grafana or integrating with enterprise observability platforms ensures that system health and performance trends are visible in real time. Proactive alerting based on predefined thresholds helps prevent overload scenarios and facilitates rapid response to anomalies.

Finally, automation and orchestration are essential tools in scaling MQTT deployments efficiently. Containerization using Docker and orchestration with Kubernetes or other container platforms enables dynamic scaling of broker instances based on demand. Kubernetes' horizontal pod autoscaler, for example, can automatically deploy new broker pods when message traffic spikes or client connections surge. Infrastructure-as-code (IaC) tools like Terraform streamline the deployment and scaling of MQTT infrastructure across multiple cloud regions, ensuring that brokers are consistently provisioned and configured to meet operational requirements.

Scaling MQTT deployments is not solely about adding more brokers; it involves a holistic strategy that spans broker architecture, load balancing, resource tuning, storage optimization, and network design. When executed effectively, these practices empower organizations to support large-scale IoT ecosystems with millions of devices generating high-frequency data streams while maintaining performance, reliability, and cost-efficiency. As IoT continues to expand into new industries and applications, scalable MQTT deployments will remain a critical component of robust and future-proof connected systems.

Retained Messages and Use Cases

Retained messages are one of MQTT's most practical and often underappreciated features, designed to improve the behavior of systems where clients frequently connect and disconnect or where new clients need to immediately receive the most recent state of a topic. In standard publish-subscribe systems, a subscriber will only receive messages that are published after it has subscribed to a topic. This means that any critical information published before the subscription was established may be lost or unavailable to new clients. Retained messages resolve this limitation by instructing the broker to store the last retained message for a specific topic and deliver it immediately to any client that subscribes to that topic thereafter.

When a publisher sends a message with the retain flag set to true, the MQTT broker stores the message along with the topic name. The next time a client subscribes to the topic, the broker sends this retained message to the subscriber as if it were just published, even if the original publishing client is no longer online. The retained message stays available until another retained message with the same topic is published to replace it, or until a retained message with an empty payload is sent to clear it. This mechanism creates a snapshot of the last known state on that topic, reducing the need for redundant communications and improving the user experience for subscribers.

One of the most common use cases for retained messages is in device status reporting. In IoT environments, devices often need to communicate their online or offline status to management systems. For example, a smart thermostat might publish a retained message to the topic home/thermostat1/status with a payload of online whenever it connects. The retained message ensures that any system monitoring device availability immediately knows that the thermostat is currently online when it subscribes to that topic. If the thermostat disconnects unexpectedly and the broker is configured to publish a Last Will and Testament message to the same topic with offline as the payload, this new retained message will replace the old one, maintaining an accurate reflection of the device's status for future subscribers.

Another powerful application of retained messages is in home automation systems. Imagine a smart lighting system where a wall-mounted control panel subscribes to various light status topics to display the current on/off state of lights in different rooms. Without retained messages, the panel would only show updates for changes that happen after it subscribes, potentially leaving the user with incomplete information about the current lighting state. By publishing retained messages such as home/livingroom/light1/status with the latest state, whether on or off, the broker ensures that as soon as the control panel connects and subscribes, it receives the last known status of each light without requiring the light switches or bulbs to re-publish their state.

Retained messages also enhance user experience in remote monitoring and dashboard applications. For example, a cloud-based dashboard designed to visualize temperature readings from multiple locations can benefit significantly from retained messages. As sensors publish temperature data with the retain flag, the broker ensures that any time the dashboard connects and subscribes to the topic farm1/fieldA/temperature, it immediately receives the most recent temperature value without waiting for the next sensor reading. This is especially helpful in systems where sensors only report data at specific intervals or when triggered by specific events.

In industrial automation, retained messages help supervisory control and data acquisition (SCADA) systems or distributed control systems (DCS) maintain up-to-date views of plant floor conditions. Actuators, machinery, or safety devices can publish their operational status or last known error codes to retained topics, enabling operators to instantly understand the system state upon launching the control interface. For example, a pump in a chemical processing plant might publish a retained message with payload running to the topic plant1/line3/pump7/status, ensuring that monitoring applications always show the latest status, even if the application starts up after the pump is already operating.

Retained messages can also simplify automation logic in event-driven systems. Automation engines and rule-based systems can subscribe to retained topics to make decisions based on the current state of devices or sensors. For instance, a smart irrigation controller might rely on retained soil moisture readings from various zones in a vineyard. When the controller subscribes to topics such as vineyard/zone4/soil_moisture, it receives the latest retained reading immediately and can decide whether to initiate irrigation without waiting for the next sensor update. This capability reduces delays in automation workflows and helps optimize resource usage.

While retained messages are a valuable tool, they must be used thoughtfully to avoid unintended consequences. In high-frequency telemetry applications, retained messages may lead to excessive broker memory usage if large retained payloads are published to numerous unique topics. Additionally, retained messages should only be used when the last known value has meaningful relevance to new subscribers. Publishing retained messages to topics with constantly changing values, such as high-frequency sensor readings, can lead to stale data being delivered to new clients if the time between data updates is long.

To mitigate such risks, MQTT system designers often implement policies around when and where to use retained messages. For example, retained messages may be limited to topics representing device statuses, configuration settings, or infrequent but critical sensor data. MQTT brokers can also be configured with limits on retained message payload sizes or topic hierarchies eligible for retained messages to manage resource consumption and system performance.

In more advanced systems, retained messages work in tandem with session persistence and Quality of Service levels to ensure reliable data delivery across distributed networks. When combined with QoS 1 or QoS 2, retained messages provide even stronger delivery guarantees, ensuring that new subscribers not only receive the last known state but also benefit from delivery acknowledgment mechanisms.

Retained messages provide a simple yet powerful way to maintain state awareness in MQTT systems. They reduce complexity for client applications, eliminate the need for redundant data publishing, and improve the responsiveness of dashboards, monitoring tools, and automation engines. Whether used for reporting device statuses, synchronizing automation logic, or enhancing the user experience in control panels, retained messages serve as an essential feature for creating efficient and state-aware IoT and distributed messaging systems. By leveraging this capability effectively, developers can build systems that are more reliable, responsive, and easier to manage across a wide range of industries and applications.

Bridging MQTT Brokers

In large-scale or geographically distributed IoT systems, it is common to encounter scenarios where a single MQTT broker is insufficient to meet operational requirements. Factors such as network segmentation, multi-site deployments, and the need for load distribution often call for multiple brokers working in concert. Bridging MQTT brokers is a solution that allows two or more MQTT brokers to be interconnected, enabling messages published to topics on one broker to be forwarded and made available on another. This creates a federated network of brokers that can share messages while maintaining autonomy within their local domains.

Broker bridging is particularly useful when organizations need to integrate multiple IoT environments that operate in distinct regions or under different administrative domains. For example, a multinational company may have separate MQTT brokers deployed at manufacturing facilities in different countries. By bridging these brokers, data from each location can be shared with a centralized broker or with other facilities, enabling unified monitoring, reporting, and analytics across the entire organization. This setup ensures that locally critical messages are processed near the source to reduce latency, while important data can still be relayed to remote sites or corporate headquarters when necessary.

The bridging mechanism works by establishing a persistent MQTT client connection between two brokers. One broker is configured to act as a bridge client, connecting to the target broker as if it were a normal MQTT client. The bridge subscribes to specific topic patterns on the local broker and republishes those messages to the remote broker, where they appear under the same or a remapped topic hierarchy. Bridging can be configured to be unidirectional, where messages flow from one broker to another, or bidirectional, where both brokers share data with each other.

One of the key benefits of bridging MQTT brokers is the ability to reduce network congestion and improve fault tolerance. In geographically distributed deployments, brokers positioned closer to devices can act as local hubs, aggregating and managing data at the edge of the network. Instead of having thousands of edge devices communicate directly with a cloud-hosted broker, they can connect to a nearby broker that handles local messaging and only forwards essential data upstream to cloud services via a bridge. This model minimizes bandwidth usage on wide-area networks, reduces message delivery latency for local clients, and maintains functionality even when internet connectivity is intermittent or unavailable.

Another advantage of bridging is the segmentation of topic spaces. In complex IoT systems with multiple teams, applications, or business units, it may be desirable to separate messaging domains for security, management, or regulatory compliance reasons. By deploying separate brokers for each domain and selectively bridging specific topics between them, organizations can enforce data isolation while still allowing critical information to flow between systems as needed. For example, a logistics company might maintain separate brokers for warehouse management and vehicle tracking, bridging only specific status updates or alerts from vehicles into the warehouse system for synchronized operations.

MQTT brokers can also be bridged in hybrid cloud and edge computing architectures. In such setups, edge brokers located within factories, hospitals, or smart buildings collect real-time data and handle local automation tasks. These brokers are bridged to cloud-hosted brokers to provide centralized visibility and long-term data storage. Sensitive data or time-critical control messages can remain within the local broker, ensuring compliance with data privacy regulations or operational requirements, while non-critical telemetry is shared with cloud analytics services.

However, implementing broker bridging requires careful planning to avoid common pitfalls such as message loops and duplicate data. Message loops occur when two brokers are configured to bridge the same set of topics bidirectionally without appropriate filtering. A message published to broker A could be forwarded to broker B and then bridged back to broker A, resulting in an infinite loop of redundant traffic. To prevent this, brokers typically support topic remapping or loop detection mechanisms that tag forwarded messages to avoid retransmission to their origin.

Another consideration is message ordering and Quality of Service (QoS) handling. When bridging brokers, messages may traverse multiple network segments and broker hops, increasing the chances of out-of-order delivery or duplicate messages if QoS 1 or QoS 2 levels are used. Systems relying on strict message ordering may need additional logic at the application layer to handle reordering or deduplication. Additionally, bridged brokers must be configured to preserve QoS levels where required, ensuring that message delivery guarantees remain intact across the bridged connection.

Security is also a key factor when bridging brokers across networks or administrative domains. The bridging connection itself should be secured using TLS to encrypt data in transit. Furthermore, proper authentication and authorization policies must be enforced on both the local and remote brokers to prevent unauthorized access to sensitive topics or system functions. Some MQTT brokers allow fine-grained control over which topics can be bridged and under what conditions, helping administrators enforce strict data governance and compliance measures.

Scalability is another consideration when deploying broker bridges. While bridging can extend the reach of MQTT networks, it introduces additional traffic to the brokers involved. In high-volume environments, this may necessitate load balancing and clustering strategies to prevent individual brokers from becoming overloaded. It may also require optimizing topic filters to ensure that only relevant data is bridged between brokers, reducing unnecessary load and improving system performance.

Broker bridging is frequently used to integrate MQTT with non-MQTT systems as well. A broker in one region may act as a bridge to relay MQTT messages to an enterprise service bus (ESB) or an event streaming platform like Apache Kafka via dedicated connectors. This architecture allows MQTT to serve as the data collection layer at the edge, while other systems handle long-term processing, analytics, and integration with business applications.

Ultimately, bridging MQTT brokers extends the flexibility and scalability of MQTT networks, enabling architects to build distributed and hierarchical communication systems tailored to specific operational, geographic, or security requirements. By leveraging bridges effectively, organizations can create interconnected broker networks that support seamless data exchange, optimized resource usage, and resilient system architectures. Whether connecting remote sites, segmenting applications, or unifying cloud and edge environments, broker bridging plays a pivotal role in expanding the reach and functionality of MQTT-powered IoT ecosystems.

MQTT and Data Analytics Pipelines

In modern IoT ecosystems, the ability to collect, process, and analyze large volumes of real-time data has become a fundamental requirement for organizations aiming to drive operational efficiency, improve decision-making, and uncover actionable insights. MQTT, with its lightweight messaging architecture, serves as an ideal transport protocol for ingesting telemetry data from thousands or millions of connected devices into data analytics pipelines. MQTT's publish-subscribe model, combined with its minimal network overhead and support for asynchronous communication, makes it well-suited for feeding real-time data streams directly into powerful analytics systems.

At the core of this integration is MQTT's role as the data ingestion layer. IoT devices deployed across industries such as manufacturing, transportation, healthcare, agriculture, and smart cities continuously publish sensor readings, status updates, and event notifications to MQTT brokers. These brokers, acting as centralized hubs, collect data from distributed edge devices and facilitate its flow into downstream analytics platforms. MQTT's ability to handle diverse message payloads—ranging from simple numerical readings to complex JSON or binary data—allows for flexibility in the types of data that can be processed by analytics pipelines.

Once collected by the MQTT broker, the data needs to be routed to processing engines or storage systems capable of handling high-velocity data streams. In many architectures, MQTT brokers integrate directly with event streaming platforms such as Apache Kafka, Amazon Kinesis, or Google Cloud Pub/Sub. These platforms provide distributed, scalable infrastructures designed to process millions of messages per second. MQTT brokers can be configured with built-in or custom connectors that automatically forward incoming messages to these systems, bridging the gap between device-level telemetry and enterprise-grade data processing.

In an industrial IoT deployment, for example, sensors installed on a production line might publish vibration data, temperature readings, and machine status updates to an MQTT broker. The broker, through a connector, streams this data into a Kafka topic partitioned by machine ID or production line. Downstream consumers, such as data processing frameworks built on Apache Flink or Spark Streaming, then consume the data in real time to perform complex event processing, anomaly detection, or predictive maintenance modeling. The insights generated from this pipeline can trigger automated actions, such as sending alerts to maintenance teams, adjusting machine settings, or logging data to an enterprise resource planning (ERP) system.

Edge-to-cloud architectures also benefit from MQTT's integration with analytics pipelines. Edge brokers deployed in factories, warehouses, or remote facilities aggregate local data and forward relevant messages to cloud-hosted data platforms. This hybrid approach allows for initial preprocessing or filtering at the edge to reduce bandwidth usage and latency, while still ensuring that critical data is made available for cloud-based analytics and machine learning services. MQTT's retained message feature can also play a role in ensuring that data snapshots or key status updates are persistently available to analytics consumers upon subscription.

For organizations operating in regulated industries or handling sensitive data, MQTT's integration with data pipelines enables selective data routing. Security policies may dictate that certain data streams, such as personally identifiable information (PII) or financial records, are processed within private data centers, while anonymized telemetry is forwarded to public cloud analytics services. MQTT brokers can be configured to segregate topics and route messages based on business rules, ensuring compliance with regulations while optimizing data flow efficiency.

Real-time dashboards and visualization platforms are another component of data analytics pipelines that benefit from MQTT integration. MQTT messages can be consumed by visualization tools like Grafana, Kibana, or custom-built web applications that subscribe to MQTT topics or consume data from intermediate streaming platforms. These dashboards display key performance indicators (KPIs), sensor trends, and system health metrics, providing operators, analysts, and decision-makers with up-to-date insights. In smart city applications, for instance, MQTT-powered data pipelines may feed live traffic data, air quality indices, and public transport updates into centralized dashboards used by urban planners and emergency services.

MQTT also plays a key role in powering artificial intelligence (AI) and machine learning (ML) applications. Historical data collected via MQTT can be stored in cloud data warehouses, such as Amazon Redshift, Google BigQuery, or Snowflake, for offline analysis and model training. Once trained, ML models can be deployed within data pipelines to process incoming MQTT messages in real time, applying techniques such as classification, regression, or clustering to detect anomalies, forecast demand, or optimize operations. A retail company, for example, might use MQTT to collect foot traffic data from smart cameras and deploy ML models to predict customer behavior and dynamically adjust store layouts.

Another powerful feature of MQTT in data pipelines is its compatibility with serverless architectures. MQTT brokers can be integrated with serverless computing platforms like AWS Lambda, Azure Functions, or Google Cloud Functions, allowing developers to trigger lightweight, event-driven workflows directly in response to incoming MQTT messages. Serverless functions can enrich data, apply business logic, or route messages to external systems, all without managing dedicated infrastructure. This model supports agile, scalable pipeline architectures and simplifies the deployment of microservices tailored to specific analytics tasks.

Scalability and resilience are essential when designing MQTT-powered data pipelines. As data volume increases, broker clustering and load balancing strategies ensure that message ingestion remains efficient and reliable. Additionally, careful topic hierarchy design enables fine-grained data filtering and routing. For example, an energy utility company might organize topics by region and sensor type, such as grid/region1/transformer5/temperature, allowing analytics pipelines to focus on relevant subsets of the data for specific use cases.

Data quality management is another crucial consideration in these pipelines. MQTT's Quality of Service (QoS) levels help balance delivery guarantees with resource efficiency. QoS 0 may be used for non-critical telemetry, while QoS 1 or QoS 2 ensures delivery of high-priority messages such as system alerts or control commands. Downstream analytics pipelines often implement additional data validation and cleansing stages to detect outliers, missing values, or inconsistent data points before feeding information into analytic models or reports.

Ultimately, MQTT serves as the entry point for transforming raw IoT data into actionable intelligence within data analytics pipelines. By bridging edge devices with cloud-native services, event stream processors, and advanced analytics platforms, MQTT empowers organizations to leverage real-time data to drive automation, optimize processes, and gain deeper insights into their operations. As IoT ecosystems continue to grow in complexity and scale, MQTT's lightweight and versatile messaging architecture remains a critical component of modern data-driven solutions.

MQTT and AI/ML at the Edge

The intersection of MQTT with artificial intelligence (AI) and machine learning (ML) at the edge is reshaping how organizations design and deploy intelligent IoT systems. As the demand for real-time decision-making and localized data processing grows, edge computing has become a natural complement to centralized cloud infrastructures. MQTT, with its lightweight, efficient messaging model, serves as a vital link between edge devices, sensors, and embedded AI/ML engines. By enabling seamless communication between distributed components, MQTT facilitates the deployment of AI/ML models directly at the edge, where data is generated, unlocking faster response times and reducing dependence on cloud-based services.

Edge AI/ML refers to running AI and machine learning models on devices located physically close to the data source. These devices, which range from industrial gateways and embedded systems to microcontrollers and smart cameras, process raw sensor data locally and make decisions without needing to send large volumes of information to the cloud for analysis. This decentralized approach addresses several key challenges in modern IoT systems, including network bandwidth limitations, data privacy concerns, and the latency introduced by cloud-based processing. MQTT enhances this architecture by providing an efficient and reliable means of transporting messages between IoT devices, edge gateways, and AI/ML inference engines.

In industrial automation, AI/ML at the edge is used to implement predictive maintenance, process optimization, and quality control. Edge devices continuously collect data such as vibration levels, motor temperatures, and production line speeds, publishing this information to local MQTT brokers. AI/ML models deployed on edge servers or gateways subscribe to these MQTT topics to ingest the data streams in real time. The models then analyze the incoming data to detect anomalies, predict equipment failures, or recommend process adjustments. For instance, an AI model trained to identify abnormal vibration patterns in a rotating machine might detect early signs of mechanical wear and publish an alert message to an MQTT topic monitored by maintenance teams.

The integration of MQTT with AI/ML at the edge extends beyond manufacturing. In smart cities, edge-based AI models are embedded within traffic cameras, air quality monitors, and public safety systems. These models process video feeds or sensor data locally to identify traffic congestion, monitor pollution levels, or detect public safety incidents. The results of this analysis are published to MQTT topics and forwarded to traffic control centers, emergency response units, or city dashboards. MQTT's efficient messaging model ensures that critical insights are delivered to the right systems without overwhelming the network with raw data.

In the healthcare sector, MQTT-enabled edge devices combined with AI/ML are transforming patient monitoring and diagnostics. Wearable health monitors and medical IoT devices equipped with AI models analyze patient vitals, such as heart rate, blood pressure, and oxygen saturation, in real time. Anomalies such as arrhythmias or hypoxia can be detected locally, with actionable insights or alerts published via MQTT to hospital systems, clinician dashboards, or cloud platforms for further review. The combination of MQTT's low power consumption and AI's diagnostic capabilities allows for continuous monitoring in remote care scenarios, improving patient outcomes while reducing the load on centralized infrastructure.

Retail and logistics industries are also leveraging MQTT and AI/ML at the edge to improve operational efficiency and customer experience. Smart shelves, cameras, and IoT-enabled point-of-sale systems deploy AI models to track inventory levels, monitor customer foot traffic, and detect potential theft. These edge devices publish their observations to MQTT brokers, which distribute actionable insights to inventory management systems or security teams. In warehouse operations, autonomous robots equipped with AI navigation models subscribe to MQTT topics for real-time updates on order fulfillment priorities and warehouse layout changes, ensuring smooth coordination without cloud dependency.

The combination of MQTT with AI/ML at the edge introduces significant bandwidth savings. Instead of transmitting every sensor reading, image, or video frame to the cloud, edge devices run inference locally and publish only summarized data or actionable decisions via MQTT. For example, a smart camera using an AI model to detect the presence of specific objects or behaviors will only publish messages when an event of interest occurs, such as detecting a safety violation on a factory floor. This dramatically reduces the amount of data transmitted, lowers operational costs, and enhances data privacy by keeping sensitive information localized.

Security is a critical factor when deploying AI/ML models at the edge with MQTT. Devices performing AI inference may process sensitive data, such as video feeds or patient health metrics. MQTT provides a secure transport layer through TLS encryption, while additional security measures such as device authentication, access control lists (ACLs), and secure edge hardware with trusted execution environments (TEEs) protect data integrity and confidentiality. Furthermore, MQTT's session management and Quality of Service (QoS) settings help ensure that critical AI-generated messages, such as alerts or control commands, are reliably delivered to subscribers even in unreliable or constrained network environments.

The flexibility of MQTT's topic hierarchy is well-suited to AI/ML workflows at the edge. Topics can be structured to organize AI-generated outputs, device telemetry, and control messages in a logical manner. In a fleet management application, edge devices embedded in vehicles might publish to topics such as fleet/truck7/ai_predictions/collision_risk, while subscribing to fleet/truck7/commands for navigation adjustments based on remote AI analysis or centralized fleet management decisions. This publish-subscribe model supports both local autonomy and coordinated decision-making across distributed systems.

Model management and lifecycle deployment also benefit from MQTT integration. AI/ML models deployed at the edge need to be regularly updated to incorporate new training data, adapt to changing conditions, or improve performance. MQTT can facilitate model distribution and updates by serving as a communication channel between edge nodes and central management systems. For instance, when a new AI model version is available, a message can be published to an MQTT topic subscribed to by edge devices, triggering an automated model download and deployment process.

As edge hardware continues to evolve, the synergy between MQTT and AI/ML will only grow stronger. New generations of AI accelerators, such as NVIDIA Jetson modules or Google Coral Edge TPUs, provide powerful inference capabilities in compact, energy-efficient form factors. When paired with MQTT brokers running locally or on nearby gateways, these devices enable sophisticated AI/ML models to process high-frequency data streams directly at the edge, supporting use cases such as autonomous vehicles, intelligent surveillance, and smart manufacturing.

The ability to act on data where it is created, combined with MQTT's efficient messaging infrastructure, empowers organizations to develop highly responsive, secure, and scalable edge AI systems. By reducing cloud dependencies, lowering latency, and improving resilience, MQTT and AI/ML at the edge are shaping the future of intelligent distributed systems across industries worldwide. This architecture enables businesses to unlock the full potential of their IoT investments by turning raw edge data into real-time insights and autonomous actions that drive innovation and operational excellence.

Monitoring and Debugging MQTT Systems

The deployment of MQTT systems in production environments requires continuous monitoring and effective debugging strategies to ensure reliability, performance, and smooth operation. MQTT's lightweight and asynchronous communication model is designed to handle large volumes of data from distributed IoT devices, but without proper observability and diagnostics in place, system failures or performance degradation can go unnoticed until they cause significant disruptions. To maintain a robust and resilient MQTT system, administrators and developers must implement comprehensive monitoring frameworks that provide visibility into broker performance, client behavior, network health, and message flow.

One of the foundational aspects of monitoring MQTT systems is broker-level observability. The MQTT broker is the core of the system, handling message routing, client connections, authentication, and session management. Monitoring metrics such as the total number of active client connections, connection rates, and disconnections per unit of time can provide valuable insights into broker load and usage patterns. Sudden spikes in connection counts or persistent disconnection trends may indicate underlying issues with client-side configurations, network instability, or capacity limitations at the broker level.

Message throughput is another critical metric. Brokers should expose statistics on the number of messages published, delivered, and retained over specific time intervals. High publish rates without corresponding delivery rates could point to problems in the broker's message distribution logic or suggest that subscribers are not effectively receiving or processing messages. Tracking topic-level metrics also helps administrators understand which topics are generating the most traffic, allowing them to optimize topic hierarchies and apply quality of service (QoS) policies effectively.

In addition to message volume, monitoring message payload sizes is important. Excessively large payloads from certain devices may introduce network bottlenecks or cause broker memory usage to spike unexpectedly. Implementing message size limits or policies to compress data before publishing helps reduce these risks. Brokers that support payload inspection features can provide visibility into average payload sizes and detect anomalies where devices deviate from normal publishing patterns.

Latency and round-trip time measurements are essential for real-time applications that depend on low message delivery delays. By measuring the time between message publication and delivery to subscribers, organizations can identify network congestion or processing bottlenecks within the broker. Persistent latency spikes may signal overloaded broker instances, suboptimal network paths, or inefficient client implementations. Distributed MQTT systems with brokers in different geographic locations should also monitor cross-region latency to ensure that messages bridged between brokers meet acceptable performance thresholds.

Monitoring client behavior provides another layer of observability. Brokers often log client connection information, including client IDs, IP addresses, connection durations, keep-alive intervals, and protocol versions. These logs help detect patterns such as frequent reconnections, which might be caused by incorrect keep-alive configurations, unstable network links, or application-level logic errors. Identifying problematic clients early allows administrators to isolate issues before they impact the stability of the entire system.

Advanced MQTT brokers integrate with centralized logging and monitoring platforms such as Prometheus, Grafana, or ELK stacks (Elasticsearch, Logstash, and Kibana). These integrations enable the collection and visualization of broker metrics, system logs, and alerting rules in a unified dashboard. Administrators can create custom dashboards to monitor specific metrics such as broker CPU and memory utilization, active sessions, slow subscriptions, and message drop rates. Real-time alerts can be configured to notify operators when metrics breach defined thresholds, such as when broker memory usage exceeds 80 percent or when the number of undelivered messages exceeds expected baselines.

Debugging MQTT systems requires tools and techniques that provide deep insights into the message flows and interactions between clients and brokers. One common tool used by developers and system operators is an MQTT client simulator, which can act as both a publisher and a subscriber to test broker behavior under controlled conditions. These tools allow users to simulate thousands of virtual clients publishing or subscribing to topics, making it easier to detect broker limitations, topic filter mismatches, or message processing delays.

Packet capture tools such as Wireshark are valuable for inspecting MQTT traffic at the network layer. By analyzing MQTT control packets—such as CONNECT, PUBLISH, SUBSCRIBE, and DISCONNECT—engineers can identify malformed packets, incorrect QoS usage, or retransmission issues. In environments where TLS encryption is used, Wireshark can still provide insights into session establishment, certificate validation, and encrypted traffic patterns, even if the message payload itself is not directly viewable.

Broker logs are indispensable for debugging authentication and authorization issues. When clients fail to connect due to invalid credentials or insufficient topic permissions, brokers typically generate detailed logs indicating the cause of the failure. These logs can reveal misconfigured ACLs, expired certificates, or unsupported protocol versions. Debugging these issues at the broker level ensures that security policies are enforced without inadvertently blocking legitimate clients.

Another important consideration is monitoring retained messages and persistent sessions. Brokers should expose metrics related to the number of retained messages stored, their memory footprint, and client session persistence states. Excessive growth in retained messages may indicate poor topic management or misconfigured publisher logic, leading to resource exhaustion. Similarly, debugging persistent sessions involves ensuring that message queues for disconnected clients are being managed appropriately, with stale or unused session data cleared periodically to maintain system performance.

Message tracing is a powerful technique for end-to-end debugging. Some MQTT brokers and middleware platforms offer built-in tracing functionality, allowing administrators to follow the lifecycle of a specific message as it moves from the publisher through the broker to one or more subscribers. Message tracing provides transparency into message routing, delivery delays, and potential bottlenecks, making it easier to identify and resolve performance issues in complex deployments with multiple brokers or network segments.

MQTT bridges and edge-to-cloud architectures require special attention when monitoring and debugging. Metrics related to bridge link status, message replication rates, and synchronization latency between brokers help ensure that distributed systems operate as intended. Bridging issues, such as message loops or topic filter misconfigurations, can often be identified by analyzing the volume of bridged traffic or detecting duplicate message patterns within subscriber applications.

Security-related monitoring is also critical in MQTT deployments. Administrators should implement intrusion detection mechanisms to detect unusual patterns, such as excessive failed authentication attempts, unauthorized subscription requests, or clients publishing messages to sensitive topics without proper permissions. Combining MQTT broker logs with security information and event management

(SIEM) tools can help identify potential security threats or misconfigurations that could compromise system integrity.

Maintaining a healthy and high-performing MQTT system requires a continuous commitment to observability and a structured approach to debugging. By leveraging monitoring tools, detailed metrics, and systematic diagnostic techniques, organizations can proactively detect anomalies, resolve issues quickly, and optimize their MQTT deployments to meet the needs of modern IoT applications. As MQTT continues to serve as a key enabler of real-time communication across industries, comprehensive monitoring and debugging practices will remain essential to ensure the resilience, security, and efficiency of connected systems.

MQTT Logging and Diagnostics

Logging and diagnostics are vital components of any MQTT-based system, as they provide the necessary transparency into broker operations, client activities, and message flow that administrators and developers need to maintain system reliability and performance. Without an effective logging and diagnostic strategy, detecting subtle system anomalies, understanding communication breakdowns, and optimizing performance become extremely difficult. MQTT, as a lightweight and high-performance messaging protocol, is designed to handle large numbers of connections and high message throughput, but even the most efficient systems require detailed operational insights to ensure smooth and predictable behavior under varying workloads.

At the core of MQTT logging is the MQTT broker itself, which generates logs that capture essential information about its internal processes and interactions with connected clients. Basic logs typically include records of client connections and disconnections, authentication attempts, topic subscriptions and unsubscriptions, and message publishing events. These logs serve as a chronological record of system activity and are the first place administrators turn when troubleshooting connectivity or messaging issues.

For instance, when a client fails to connect due to invalid credentials or incorrect configuration, the broker's log will typically generate a clear message identifying the cause, such as failed password authentication or TLS handshake failure. This information enables rapid troubleshooting, especially in environments where security is tightly enforced, and access controls are granular. Likewise, if a device repeatedly disconnects and reconnects due to network instability or keep-alive timeout misconfigurations, the broker logs will highlight this behavior, allowing engineers to pinpoint the issue and take corrective action.

Beyond basic connection and authentication records, MQTT logs can be configured to capture more detailed diagnostics. Debug-level logs, when enabled, provide a deeper look into the broker's internal logic, including the processing of control packets such as CONNECT, PUBLISH, SUBSCRIBE, UNSUBSCRIBE, and DISCONNECT messages. These packet-level logs are invaluable for diagnosing client-side implementation errors, such as clients attempting to subscribe to malformed topic filters or publishing messages with unsupported Quality of Service (QoS) levels. Debug logs also help developers trace specific message flows through the system, ensuring that client applications are behaving according to the MQTT specification.

Some advanced MQTT brokers include support for message auditing, which provides detailed records of the payloads and metadata associated with messages as they pass through the system. While payload inspection must be handled with care due to privacy and compliance concerns, auditing can be essential in regulated industries where full traceability of message transactions is required. Auditing capabilities allow organizations to track the flow of critical messages, such as control commands or financial transactions, ensuring that message delivery is both reliable and compliant with operational standards.

Diagnostics in MQTT systems extend beyond logs alone. Brokers often expose diagnostic metrics through administrative dashboards or APIs, providing real-time visibility into system performance. Metrics such as broker uptime, CPU usage, memory utilization, active client connections, and message publish rates enable operators to monitor broker health and resource consumption. When combined with logs, these metrics provide a comprehensive picture of system behavior and help identify patterns that could indicate impending failures, such as memory leaks, slow subscribers, or overloaded brokers.

Effective diagnostics also rely on structured log management. In distributed MQTT systems with multiple brokers deployed across different regions or edge locations, centralized log aggregation tools are commonly used to consolidate logs from all brokers into a unified platform. Solutions such as the ELK stack (Elasticsearch, Logstash, and Kibana) or modern observability tools like Grafana Loki enable organizations to index, search, and visualize MQTT broker logs alongside metrics and application-level logs. Centralized logging simplifies root cause analysis by correlating events from different brokers, clients, and network segments.

Structured logging, where log entries are formatted in JSON or another machine-readable format, further enhances diagnostic capabilities by allowing logs to be parsed automatically by monitoring and alerting systems. For example, a structured log might record a client disconnection event along with associated metadata such as the client ID, IP address, reason code, and timestamp. This level of detail allows administrators to build dashboards and set alerts for specific patterns, such as a sudden increase in authentication failures or a surge in client disconnections in a specific geographic region.

Network-level diagnostics are equally important, especially in IoT environments where MQTT clients may operate over unreliable or low-bandwidth links. Packet capture tools such as Wireshark enable detailed analysis of MQTT traffic at the network layer. By capturing and inspecting MQTT control packets, engineers can identify retransmissions, handshake failures, and QoS mismatches between publishers and subscribers. Wireshark also provides insights into the performance of secure MQTT connections (MQTTS) by highlighting TLS handshake times, cipher suite negotiation, and session establishment latencies.

Diagnostics should also encompass retained messages and session persistence. Mismanagement of retained messages can lead to brokers consuming excessive memory or delivering outdated information to new subscribers. MQTT brokers often include tools or commands to list active retained messages, delete retained messages for specific topics, and monitor the total size of the retained message store. Regular audits of retained message usage help maintain broker efficiency and ensure that the system delivers accurate and relevant information to clients.

Another essential aspect of diagnostics is understanding QoS delivery paths. Brokers should provide insight into the behavior of QoS 1 and QoS 2 messages, including logs that detail when acknowledgment packets such as PUBACK or PUBREC are sent and received. Diagnosing message loss or duplication issues often requires correlating these logs with client-side logs, confirming that publishers and subscribers are correctly handling retries and acknowledgments as specified by the MQTT protocol.

Security-related logging is a critical part of MQTT diagnostics, especially in environments where data confidentiality and integrity are paramount. Logs capturing failed authentication attempts, authorization denials, TLS certificate errors, and unusual subscription patterns can provide early warning of potential security threats. Integration with security information and event management (SIEM) tools enables organizations to apply advanced analytics and threat detection to MQTT logs, helping to identify anomalies such as brute-force login attempts or clients attempting to subscribe to unauthorized topics.

Maintaining detailed, well-structured logs and diagnostic metrics is not only essential for resolving technical issues but also for optimizing system performance. By continuously analyzing logs, administrators can identify underutilized broker resources, eliminate redundant topic structures, and fine-tune QoS policies. This proactive approach improves system resilience and reduces operational costs while ensuring that MQTT-powered IoT ecosystems meet the growing demands of modern applications.

In highly dynamic environments such as smart cities, industrial automation, and connected transportation systems, MQTT logging and diagnostics form the foundation of reliable, scalable, and secure operations. They provide the visibility needed to maintain system integrity, optimize message flow, and quickly resolve unexpected issues, ensuring that connected devices and services perform flawlessly across diverse and distributed networks.

MQTT in Real-Time Applications

MQTT has become one of the most reliable protocols for enabling real-time applications across diverse industries, thanks to its low-latency, lightweight nature and its ability to efficiently distribute messages over constrained or high-latency networks. Real-time applications require fast and consistent communication between devices and systems, often in situations where milliseconds can make the difference between success and failure. MQTT is specifically designed to deliver small packets of information quickly and reliably, making it ideal for real-time scenarios such as industrial automation, smart cities, connected vehicles, and emergency response systems.

The publish-subscribe model of MQTT plays a crucial role in enabling real-time communication. Unlike traditional client-server communication protocols, where clients must repeatedly poll servers for updates, MQTT's broker-based model allows devices to publish data as soon as it is available. Subscribers listening to specific topics receive these updates immediately after they are published, enabling a true event-driven communication architecture. This eliminates unnecessary delays and network overhead associated with frequent polling and ensures that systems react to changes in near real-time.

In industrial environments, real-time responsiveness is critical for maintaining safety, efficiency, and productivity. Manufacturing plants rely on supervisory control and data acquisition (SCADA) systems and programmable logic controllers (PLCs) to manage complex assembly lines and automated processes. MQTT is frequently deployed within these environments to facilitate rapid communication between machines and monitoring systems. For example, if a temperature sensor on a production line detects overheating, it can publish an MQTT message to a broker with immediate effect. The message, received by a subscriber controlling the cooling system or alarm mechanism, triggers an automatic response within milliseconds to prevent equipment damage or production downtime.

In connected vehicle networks, MQTT is also used to support real-time applications such as telematics, fleet management, and vehicle-to-infrastructure (V2I) communication. Vehicles equipped with MQTT clients transmit telemetry data, including location, speed, fuel levels, and engine diagnostics, to fleet management platforms in real time. This information allows operators to optimize routes, monitor driver behavior, and coordinate logistics on the fly. Additionally, traffic management systems can use MQTT to relay critical updates, such as accident notifications or dynamic speed limits, directly to vehicles, enabling timely adjustments and safer road conditions. The low bandwidth requirements of MQTT are especially important for mobile networks, where cellular coverage may be variable and data costs can escalate quickly.

Another area where MQTT shines in real-time applications is within smart city infrastructures. Systems that monitor and control traffic signals, street lighting, waste management, and public transport all require fast and reliable communication. MQTT is leveraged to deliver instant updates to control centers and automation systems. For example, smart traffic lights can subscribe to MQTT topics that broadcast traffic density data from nearby sensors, enabling dynamic adjustment of signal timings to alleviate congestion. Similarly, connected streetlights may publish power consumption and fault status messages to a central broker, allowing operators to identify outages or inefficiencies as they occur.

Emergency response systems also benefit from MQTT's real-time capabilities. Public safety networks often integrate sensors, alarms, and communication devices to respond to emergencies quickly. Fire alarms, intrusion detection systems, and personal safety wearables can use MQTT to immediately broadcast alerts to security teams, first responders, or centralized monitoring centers. By ensuring that critical information, such as the location of an incident or sensor activation details, is transmitted instantly, MQTT enables faster response times and improved coordination in life-threatening situations.

Healthcare is another domain where real-time communication is essential, and MQTT provides an efficient backbone for modern medical IoT (IoMT) applications. In hospitals, wearable devices and patient monitoring equipment continuously collect vital signs, such as heart rate, blood pressure, and blood oxygen levels. These devices publish MQTT messages to brokers, where healthcare staff or automated systems subscribe to receive immediate updates. If an abnormal reading is detected, the system can trigger alerts, initiate medical interventions, or escalate notifications to relevant personnel without delay. In critical care units, where every second counts, MQTT ensures that doctors and nurses receive timely information that can influence life-saving decisions.

In gaming and entertainment, MQTT is used to enhance real-time interactions in multiplayer gaming platforms, live event streaming, and interactive digital experiences. Game servers use MQTT to relay player positions, actions, and in-game events to other players in real time. The lightweight nature of MQTT minimizes network latency, allowing for smooth and synchronized gameplay experiences. In large-scale live events or esports competitions, MQTT can be used to distribute instant updates, notifications, or audience engagement messages to apps and devices used by spectators and participants.

Real-time applications also extend into the realm of energy management and smart grids. Utilities require fast and efficient communication between power generation units, substations, and grid management systems to balance supply and demand in real time. MQTT supports energy monitoring and load balancing applications by facilitating rapid exchange of data such as grid frequency, power consumption, and generation output. This enables automated responses such as activating reserve generation units, shedding non-critical loads, or redistributing energy across the grid to maintain stability.

MQTT's flexibility in supporting both TCP and WebSocket transports further enhances its suitability for real-time applications. WebSocket support is particularly valuable for integrating MQTT with web-based dashboards and control panels, allowing operators to monitor and interact with systems from any location using standard web browsers. WebSocket connections maintain persistent, bidirectional communication channels, ensuring that updates from the MQTT broker reach web clients instantly without the need for repeated HTTP requests.

The protocol's support for varying QoS levels also contributes to its ability to meet different real-time requirements. In scenarios where speed is prioritized over guaranteed delivery, such as rapidly updating sensor dashboards, QoS 0 can be used to minimize latency. In contrast, for critical control messages or alarms, QoS 1 or QoS 2 ensures that messages are acknowledged and delivered reliably, even under challenging network conditions.

Security considerations remain paramount in real-time MQTT applications. As data travels quickly between devices and systems, ensuring that it is protected from unauthorized access and tampering is essential. MQTT supports TLS encryption to secure message transport, while authentication mechanisms such as username-password pairs, client certificates, and access control lists (ACLs) ensure that only authorized clients can publish or subscribe to specific topics. In real-time systems where uptime and data integrity are vital, these security measures help maintain trust and compliance with industry standards.

Overall, MQTT's design characteristics—low overhead, efficient publish-subscribe model, flexible QoS support, and ability to operate on unreliable networks—make it one of the most effective protocols for real-time applications. Its adoption across industries underscores its capability to enable fast, reliable, and scalable communication, supporting use cases where immediate responsiveness and high system availability are non-negotiable. From factories and hospitals to highways and smart grids, MQTT continues to serve as a critical enabler of real-time digital transformation.

MQTT in Disaster Recovery Scenarios

Disaster recovery planning is a critical component for ensuring business continuity and system resilience in the face of unexpected failures, natural disasters, cyber-attacks, or infrastructure disruptions. MQTT, with its lightweight and robust messaging architecture, plays a key role in enabling rapid system recovery and maintaining communication in high-risk or high-impact scenarios. As organizations increasingly rely on distributed IoT systems, MQTT has become an indispensable tool for disaster recovery strategies, ensuring that critical data continues to flow between devices, applications, and platforms even during partial system outages or total infrastructure failures.

One of MQTT's strengths in disaster recovery scenarios is its ability to operate effectively in constrained and unstable network environments. Disasters often lead to degraded network conditions, such as intermittent connectivity, high packet loss, or bandwidth limitations. MQTT was specifically designed to perform well under such conditions, making it a reliable choice for maintaining device communication in crisis situations. Its publish-subscribe model eliminates the need for devices to maintain constant two-way communication with specific endpoints, reducing the load on stressed networks and increasing the likelihood that essential messages are successfully delivered.

A key principle of disaster recovery is ensuring redundancy and failover capabilities within system architecture. MQTT supports these requirements through broker clustering and geographic distribution. In critical deployments, organizations often implement MQTT broker clusters across multiple data centers or cloud regions. These clusters are synchronized to ensure session persistence, retained messages, and client subscriptions are consistently available across different broker nodes. In the event of a data center failure, clients can automatically reconnect to brokers in other regions without loss of critical session data. This seamless failover capability is vital in disaster recovery scenarios, where minimizing downtime is essential to mitigating operational risks and financial losses.

Edge computing further enhances MQTT's role in disaster recovery. By deploying MQTT brokers at the edge, closer to the devices and sensors generating data, organizations can reduce dependency on central cloud-based systems. During a disaster, edge brokers can continue to facilitate local automation, data aggregation, and control logic, even if internet connectivity to cloud platforms is disrupted. For example, in an industrial plant experiencing a regional outage, local MQTT brokers ensure that machinery, safety systems, and monitoring equipment remain operational and autonomous while awaiting the restoration of centralized systems.

In emergency response situations, where first responders deploy temporary communication networks in the field, MQTT can be quickly integrated into mobile or ad hoc network infrastructures. MQTT brokers installed on portable servers or edge gateways enable rescue teams to establish secure and lightweight messaging frameworks for sensor networks, wearable devices, and coordination tools. Whether managing personnel safety equipment, environmental sensors, or asset tracking devices, MQTT allows responders to maintain situational awareness and coordinate actions in real time, even in remote or disaster-stricken areas where conventional communication systems are unavailable.

Another advantage of MQTT in disaster recovery is its retained message feature. Retained messages ensure that the most recent state of critical devices or systems is always available to new subscribers, even after reconnections following a disruption. For instance, in a smart building scenario where environmental controls and alarm systems depend on MQTT communication, retained messages can be used to store the latest operational status of devices such as fire alarms, HVAC systems, and emergency lighting. If a building's control system goes offline and reconnects later, it immediately receives the last known status of these systems, facilitating faster recovery and reducing the risk of unsafe conditions.

Disaster recovery scenarios often require efficient bandwidth utilization, especially when fallback networks, such as satellite or cellular connections, are limited in capacity. MQTT's minimal packet overhead allows critical messages to be transmitted using as little bandwidth as possible, conserving network resources for essential communication. This is especially useful when coordinating field operations during natural disasters like hurricanes, earthquakes, or floods, where available network infrastructure may be damaged, congested, or dependent on temporary wireless connections.

Security is another paramount concern during disasters, as opportunistic cyber-attacks or data breaches can exploit system vulnerabilities created by chaotic conditions. MQTT supports TLS encryption to ensure that messages are protected in transit, and brokers can enforce strict authentication policies even under degraded network conditions. MQTT's topic-based access control allows organizations to limit which devices or users can publish or subscribe to sensitive data, reducing the risk of unauthorized access or data leakage during recovery operations.

MQTT's flexibility also makes it well-suited for integration with disaster recovery orchestration tools. Automated workflows can be configured to monitor MQTT broker health, connection status, and message delivery metrics. In the event of broker degradation or failure, orchestration platforms can initiate failover processes, such as rerouting MQTT traffic to standby brokers or launching additional broker instances in unaffected regions. MQTT's compatibility with containerized environments, such as Docker and Kubernetes, further simplifies the automation of disaster recovery procedures by enabling rapid deployment and scaling of broker infrastructure in response to emerging threats or failures.

In smart grid and utility networks, MQTT supports the resilience of critical infrastructure during disasters. Power grids, water treatment facilities, and gas distribution systems rely on continuous monitoring and control to prevent cascading failures or hazardous conditions. MQTT brokers located at substations or control centers collect and disseminate telemetry data from field devices, including transformer status, circuit breaker positions, and power flow measurements. If a central control center becomes unreachable, MQTT ensures that decentralized control systems and field operators still receive critical data, allowing them to make informed decisions to stabilize the grid or isolate faults.

In aviation and maritime industries, disaster recovery protocols often incorporate MQTT to support communication continuity in isolated environments. Aircraft and ships operating beyond the range of terrestrial networks may experience communication blackouts during extreme weather events or system failures. MQTT clients running on onboard devices can buffer data locally and publish to satellite-connected brokers when a link becomes available, ensuring that critical telemetry, navigation, and safety information is preserved and forwarded as soon as communication is reestablished.

Ultimately, MQTT's characteristics make it an essential component of disaster recovery strategies across a wide range of industries. Its ability to maintain lightweight, real-time communication over unreliable networks, support broker redundancy and failover, and integrate with edge and cloud infrastructures ensures that critical systems can continue to function during disruptions. Whether supporting life-saving emergency response operations, ensuring continuity in industrial control systems, or maintaining connectivity in remote and challenging environments, MQTT provides the resilience and adaptability needed to safeguard modern IoT ecosystems during times of crisis.

Energy-Efficient MQTT Designs

Designing energy-efficient MQTT systems is crucial for ensuring the sustainability and operational longevity of IoT devices, especially in remote or battery-powered applications. MQTT's inherent design is already optimized for low-bandwidth and resource-constrained environments, but to maximize energy efficiency further, architects and developers must take deliberate steps to fine-tune how MQTT is implemented across devices, brokers, and networks. Energy efficiency in MQTT deployments is not just about reducing power consumption but also about extending device uptime, reducing maintenance cycles, and enabling the deployment of systems in areas where energy supply is limited or unreliable.

One of the key principles in designing energy-efficient MQTT systems is minimizing unnecessary device wake cycles and communication overhead. Many IoT devices, particularly those deployed in remote monitoring or environmental sensing applications, operate on limited battery capacity. To conserve energy, these devices often spend most of their operational life in sleep mode, waking periodically to collect data and publish it via MQTT. Using MQTT's lightweight protocol and small packet sizes, devices can quickly establish a connection, transmit essential data, and return to sleep, reducing the power consumed by radio modules and microcontrollers. This duty-cycling approach, combined with MQTT's minimal transport overhead, significantly extends battery life compared to heavier protocols such as HTTP or AMQP.

Efficient MQTT designs also rely on intelligent use of Quality of Service levels. MQTT supports three QoS levels, each with different energy implications. QoS 0, which offers at-most-once delivery with no acknowledgment, consumes the least energy and is suitable for non-critical data such as periodic environmental readings where occasional data loss is acceptable. QoS 1 and QoS 2 introduce additional message exchanges to guarantee delivery, which, while improving reliability, increase power consumption due to the extra network activity required. Balancing QoS selection according to application criticality is essential for energy-efficient operation. For example, critical alerts from a security sensor may warrant QoS 1, while periodic telemetry from a temperature sensor might use QoS 0 to minimize energy usage.

Another important consideration is optimizing the keep-alive interval used in MQTT connections. The keep-alive setting dictates how often a client must send a PINGREQ message to the broker to maintain the connection. Longer keep-alive intervals reduce the frequency of network transmissions, conserving energy, especially in devices operating over cellular or LPWAN networks where radio modules are significant energy consumers. However, excessively long keep-alive intervals may lead to broker-side session timeouts or missed disconnection events. Striking the right balance based on network reliability and application requirements is key to optimizing energy consumption without sacrificing connection reliability.

The retained message feature of MQTT also plays a role in designing energy-efficient systems. By publishing retained messages for non-volatile data, such as system status or configuration settings, devices can avoid redundant transmissions. When a new client or system component subscribes to a topic, it immediately receives the last retained message without requiring the original publisher to send fresh data. This reduces the total number of transmissions and helps battery-powered devices conserve energy by minimizing unnecessary publishing activity.

Network topology and broker placement also affect the energy footprint of MQTT systems. Edge computing can be leveraged to reduce the distance that data travels, thus lowering the energy required for each transmission. Deploying local MQTT brokers at the network edge allows devices to communicate with nearby nodes rather than transmitting data over long distances to centralized cloud brokers. This reduces both the power draw of devices' communication modules and network congestion. In remote agricultural deployments, for example, MQTT brokers running on edge gateways within the field allow sensors to offload data locally, reducing the need for frequent high-energy cellular transmissions to cloud infrastructure.

Batching and aggregating messages is another technique for improving energy efficiency. Instead of transmitting data as soon as it is collected, devices can store readings locally and publish them in batches at set intervals. This reduces the frequency of radio transmissions, which is one of the most power-intensive activities for wireless devices. However, batching must be balanced with the latency requirements of the application. In non-time-sensitive scenarios such as long-term environmental monitoring, batching is highly effective. In contrast, real-time safety-critical systems may require immediate transmission of certain events regardless of energy cost.

Compression and lightweight data formats are additional considerations in energy-efficient MQTT design. Using compact data formats such as CBOR or MessagePack instead of verbose formats like JSON reduces the size of payloads, requiring fewer bytes to be transmitted over the network. Smaller payloads result in shorter radio transmission times, conserving energy on both the client and network sides. Compression algorithms can also be employed, but care must be taken to select algorithms that are computationally lightweight to avoid negating energy savings through excessive processing overhead on constrained devices.

Energy-aware scheduling and adaptive transmission strategies further enhance MQTT system efficiency. Devices can dynamically adjust their reporting frequency based on environmental conditions, system states, or battery levels. For example, a soil moisture sensor might increase its reporting frequency during dry conditions but reduce it when sufficient moisture is detected. MQTT's flexibility supports such dynamic behavior by allowing devices to adjust their publication rates without requiring complex reconfiguration of the broker or system infrastructure.

The role of MQTT brokers in energy-efficient systems extends to efficient session management. Brokers can be configured to manage persistent sessions for clients that operate intermittently, ensuring that messages published while the client is offline are queued and delivered when the client reconnects. This eliminates the need for devices to remain online continuously, reducing their active power consumption and enabling them to remain in sleep mode for extended periods.

Security in MQTT systems must also be approached with energy efficiency in mind. While encryption and authentication are critical, choosing lightweight security mechanisms and efficient cryptographic algorithms is important for battery-powered devices. MQTT clients can implement TLS session resumption and session caching to reduce the overhead of repeated handshakes, saving energy by shortening connection establishment times.

Energy-efficient MQTT designs are foundational to the success of large-scale IoT projects where devices are deployed in the field for years at a time without easy access to maintenance or battery replacement. From smart agriculture and wildlife tracking to environmental monitoring and smart metering, MQTT provides a highly adaptable and efficient framework for building systems that are both sustainable and resilient. By carefully optimizing MQTT configurations, adopting edge computing principles, and fine-tuning transmission strategies, engineers can significantly reduce the energy demands of IoT networks while maintaining the responsiveness and reliability required for modern connected applications.

MQTT Client Libraries in Python

Python is one of the most popular programming languages in the world, widely used for everything from web development and data science to IoT applications and embedded systems. The simplicity and flexibility of Python make it a natural fit for working with MQTT, especially in IoT ecosystems where rapid prototyping and seamless integration with cloud platforms and data pipelines are required. Python's extensive ecosystem of MQTT client libraries allows developers to easily build publishers, subscribers, and sophisticated automation systems for MQTT-based networks. The most commonly used MQTT library in Python is Paho-MQTT, maintained by the Eclipse Foundation, but several other libraries and frameworks also offer MQTT support.

The Paho-MQTT library is widely regarded as the de facto standard MQTT client for Python. It fully implements the MQTT 3.1 and 3.1.1 specifications and is actively maintained with regular updates and community support. Paho-MQTT provides a high-level API that abstracts much of the complexity involved in managing MQTT connections, subscriptions, and message handling. With just a few lines of code, developers can create a client that connects to a broker, subscribes to topics, and handles incoming messages using callback functions.

The core of working with Paho-MQTT revolves around the client object, which manages the lifecycle of an MQTT session. Developers can configure this client with parameters such as broker IP address or hostname, port number, keep-alive interval, and security settings like TLS certificates. The client provides methods for connecting to the broker, publishing messages to specific topics, subscribing to topics, and gracefully disconnecting when communication is complete. Paho-MQTT's design follows an asynchronous pattern, using callbacks for connection events, message delivery confirmations, and incoming messages. This approach allows for non-blocking, event-driven applications that are essential for responsive IoT systems.

In addition to basic functionality, Paho-MQTT supports advanced MQTT features such as retained messages, persistent sessions, and all three QoS levels. Developers can use the library to control how messages are delivered depending on system requirements, balancing trade-offs between delivery guarantees and resource efficiency. For example, a developer building a real-time dashboard application may prefer QoS 0 for non-critical updates, while using QoS 1 for publishing critical alerts that must be acknowledged by the broker.

Paho-MQTT also provides hooks for implementing security best practices. Developers can configure the client to establish secure connections to MQTT brokers using TLS, authenticate with username-password pairs, or even use client certificates for mutual TLS authentication. This is especially important when integrating Python-based applications with cloud-hosted brokers such as AWS IoT Core, Microsoft Azure IoT Hub, or Google Cloud IoT, all of which require strict authentication and encrypted communication.

Beyond Paho-MQTT, other Python libraries and frameworks offer MQTT support. One such example is asyncio-mqtt, which leverages Python's asyncio framework to provide a fully asynchronous MQTT client experience. This library is particularly well-suited for modern Python applications that make extensive use of async and await patterns to manage concurrency efficiently. By using asyncio-mqtt, developers can integrate MQTT communication into larger asynchronous applications, such as web services, data pipelines, or event-driven microservices.

Another library is HBMQTT, which implements both MQTT client and broker functionality in Python. While HBMQTT is less widely used than Paho-MQTT, it is notable for allowing developers to implement lightweight MQTT brokers directly in Python, making it useful for embedded systems, testing environments, or small-scale applications where deploying a separate broker is unnecessary. HBMQTT also provides an asynchronous client API based on asyncio, making it suitable for applications that require non-blocking behavior.

Developers working in the data science and analytics space often integrate Python MQTT clients with other tools such as pandas, NumPy, or machine learning frameworks like TensorFlow and PyTorch. This integration allows MQTT clients written in Python to act as data collectors, subscribing to sensor data from IoT devices and streaming this information directly into analytics pipelines or machine learning models. For example, a Python script using Paho-MQTT might subscribe to environmental data such as temperature and humidity from a network of sensors and then use pandas to aggregate and analyze this data in real time, providing insights that are displayed in a dashboard or used to trigger automated actions.

MQTT client libraries in Python are also commonly integrated with web frameworks such as Flask or FastAPI. In this configuration, the MQTT client can run as part of a backend web service that receives MQTT messages and then serves processed data to frontend applications via REST APIs or WebSocket connections. This is a popular design pattern for IoT dashboards, where the Python-based backend acts as a bridge between MQTT-enabled devices and user-facing applications.

Automation tools such as Home Assistant, an open-source home automation platform, heavily leverage MQTT and are built in Python. Home Assistant includes built-in MQTT integration using Python client libraries, enabling users to create highly customized smart home automations and monitoring systems that interact with a wide variety of MQTT-compatible devices such as sensors, switches, and smart appliances.

When working with MQTT client libraries in Python, developers often implement logging and diagnostic features to monitor message flow and troubleshoot connection issues. Paho-MQTT and other libraries provide options for enabling verbose logging, which records events such as connection attempts, subscription acknowledgments, message delivery statuses, and broker responses. Logging is essential for identifying issues related to network reliability, broker configurations, or client misbehavior, especially when deploying MQTT systems in production environments where resilience and uptime are critical.

Python's flexibility, combined with MQTT's efficiency, allows for rapid prototyping and deployment of IoT systems across a wide range of industries. Whether it is a developer building a simple script to automate tasks in a smart home or a team deploying a large-scale industrial IoT platform, Python's MQTT client libraries provide the necessary tools to create reliable and scalable applications. The combination of Python's clean syntax, extensive ecosystem, and MQTT's lightweight design makes them a natural pairing for IoT projects that require fast development cycles, cross-platform compatibility, and integration with cloud services and data analytics platforms.

MQTT Client Libraries in Java

Java has long been a popular programming language for developing enterprise-level applications, backend systems, and embedded solutions, making it a strong choice for building MQTT clients in IoT architectures. The language's portability, mature ecosystem, and strong community support have led to the widespread use of Java in both cloud-based applications and edge computing devices. Java's MQTT client libraries enable developers to build scalable and reliable applications that can publish and subscribe to MQTT topics, manage device communications, and process real-time data from IoT devices.

One of the most widely used MQTT client libraries in Java is Eclipse Paho, which provides a complete implementation of the MQTT protocol versions 3.1 and 3.1.1, with support for MQTT 5.0 features in more recent releases. The Eclipse Paho Java library is robust, well-documented, and designed to integrate smoothly with other components in Java-based systems. Paho's client API allows developers to manage MQTT connections, handle subscriptions, and publish messages with ease, using an object-oriented design that aligns well with Java development practices.

The Paho MQTT client in Java provides both synchronous and asynchronous APIs. The synchronous API allows developers to write straightforward, blocking code where each operation waits until it completes. This model is easy to implement in simpler applications where real-time constraints are minimal. However, many developers opt for the asynchronous API, which provides non-blocking behavior by using callbacks and listeners to handle events such as successful connections, incoming messages, and delivery confirmations. The asynchronous model is ideal for applications that require responsive, event-driven behavior, such as backend microservices or IoT gateways processing large volumes of messages in parallel.

Security is a critical component in MQTT systems, and the Paho Java client offers comprehensive support for secure communication. Developers can configure TLS/SSL settings to encrypt MQTT traffic, protecting data in transit between clients and brokers. Paho allows developers to provide custom certificates, set up mutual TLS authentication, and configure secure socket factories to comply with enterprise security policies or regulatory requirements. Additionally, the client can be configured to support username and password-based authentication or integrate with external identity providers when connecting to managed IoT services like AWS IoT Core, Azure IoT Hub, or HiveMQ Cloud.

Another key feature of the Paho Java client is its support for MQTT's Quality of Service levels, retained messages, and persistent sessions. Developers can fine-tune their applications by selecting appropriate QoS levels based on the criticality of data delivery. For instance, telemetry from non-critical sensors may use QoS 0, while important control commands or alerts may be transmitted using QoS 1 or QoS 2 to ensure reliable delivery. The library also supports retained messages, enabling the broker to store and forward the most recent message to new subscribers immediately after they connect, which is highly useful in state synchronization scenarios.

In enterprise and industrial IoT applications, Java-based clients are often integrated with other Java frameworks and technologies. For example, developers building Spring Boot applications can embed the Paho MQTT client within microservices, allowing backend components to consume data from IoT devices and forward processed information to databases, analytics platforms, or other services via RESTful APIs or event streams such as Kafka. This architecture is commonly used to create centralized IoT platforms capable of monitoring devices, running analytics, and issuing commands to edge nodes.

Another notable Java MQTT client library is Moquette, which implements an embedded MQTT broker and client, allowing developers to build self-contained applications that both publish and consume MQTT messages without relying on an external broker. Moquette is often used in edge computing scenarios where limited hardware resources or offline operation requires deploying both client and broker functionality on the same device. This embedded approach reduces network latency and can enable autonomous operations in smart factories, agricultural monitoring systems, and remote installations.

Additionally, libraries such as HiveMQ MQTT Client provide advanced features beyond the basic MQTT specification. The HiveMQ client supports MQTT 5.0 natively, which includes features such as enhanced authentication, message expiry intervals, topic aliases, and user properties. These enhancements improve performance, scalability, and flexibility in modern IoT systems. The HiveMQ client is also designed with reactive programming principles, making it a good fit for applications built using frameworks like Project Reactor or RxJava.

Java's platform independence is another major advantage when building MQTT clients, as the same codebase can run on diverse environments, from embedded devices and Android smartphones to cloud servers and enterprise data centers. This portability allows organizations to build cross-platform solutions where MQTT clients on edge devices interact seamlessly with backend systems deployed in virtualized or containerized environments in the cloud.

When building MQTT clients in Java, it is common practice to implement comprehensive logging and monitoring capabilities. Most Java MQTT client libraries, including Paho, provide hooks for integrating with Java's logging frameworks such as Log4j, SLF4J, or java.util.logging. Logging enables developers to track connection attempts, message publication outcomes, subscription activities, and broker responses, making it easier to diagnose issues in production environments. Furthermore, logs can be correlated with system metrics to identify performance bottlenecks or connection issues caused by unreliable networks or broker outages.

Java's MQTT clients are also frequently used in Android development for building IoT applications on mobile platforms. Android devices equipped with MQTT clients can subscribe to real-time updates from smart home devices, industrial sensors, or connected vehicles, providing users with instant feedback and control capabilities. The Paho Android Service, a variant of the Paho MQTT library, is tailored for use within Android applications, offering background service management to handle MQTT communication even when the app is not in the foreground.

In addition to Android, Java MQTT clients integrate smoothly with other IoT platforms, such as Eclipse Kura, an open-source IoT gateway framework also written in Java. Using Kura, developers can deploy Java-based MQTT clients at the edge to collect sensor data, perform local processing, and relay critical information to cloud-based MQTT brokers, supporting edge-to-cloud data flows in distributed IoT architectures.

Overall, Java's rich ecosystem, combined with robust MQTT client libraries, provides developers with powerful tools for building scalable, secure, and high-performance IoT solutions. Whether deployed in smart cities, industrial automation, healthcare, or transportation systems, Java MQTT clients offer the flexibility and reliability needed to bridge edge devices, cloud platforms, and enterprise systems within modern IoT ecosystems.

MQTT Client Libraries in C/C++

C and C++ remain among the most widely used programming languages for building embedded systems, IoT devices, and performance-critical applications, making them essential for implementing MQTT clients in resource-constrained environments. Many edge devices, including sensors, microcontrollers, and gateways, operate with limited processing power and memory, requiring efficient communication protocols and lightweight client libraries. MQTT, being specifically designed for low-bandwidth and high-latency networks, pairs exceptionally well with C and C++ due to their ability to produce highly optimized and portable code that runs directly on bare-metal hardware or embedded operating systems.

One of the most prominent MQTT client libraries for C and C++ is Eclipse Paho C Client. This library provides a full implementation of the MQTT 3.1 and 3.1.1 protocols and supports both synchronous and asynchronous APIs. The synchronous API is straightforward to use and appropriate for applications where blocking behavior is acceptable, while the asynchronous API allows developers to build non-blocking applications using callbacks and event-driven logic, which is essential for embedded devices that need to handle multiple tasks simultaneously.

The Paho C Client library is written in pure C, ensuring that it can be compiled and executed on a wide range of embedded platforms, from Linux-based systems such as Raspberry Pi to real-time operating systems (RTOS) like FreeRTOS or Zephyr. Because it is written in C, the library has a very small memory footprint and does not rely on heavyweight runtime dependencies, making it ideal for microcontrollers and embedded processors with constrained resources. Developers can use this library to easily create MQTT clients that connect to brokers, subscribe to topics, publish messages, and manage disconnections in systems where every kilobyte of memory matters.

For applications requiring MQTT 5.0 support, Eclipse Paho C++ Client is another option. This library is a C++ wrapper built on top of the Paho C Client, providing a more modern and object-oriented interface for C++ developers. It enables the use of C++ programming paradigms such as RAII (Resource Acquisition Is Initialization), smart pointers, and standard library containers, making the code more maintainable and expressive. With the C++ client, developers can take advantage of additional MQTT 5.0 features such as session expiry intervals, topic aliases, user properties, and enhanced error reporting.

Security is a crucial consideration when building MQTT clients in C and C++ for IoT applications. Both the Paho C and C++ clients support TLS encryption through integration with libraries such as OpenSSL or mbedTLS. This allows developers to create secure MQTT clients that authenticate with brokers using certificates, ensure message confidentiality through encryption, and prevent man-in-the-middle attacks. Additionally, username and password authentication can be configured to provide basic security for non-critical applications or when working in trusted network environments.

Another widely used C-based MQTT client library is Eclipse Mosquitto Client Library. Originally developed as part of the Mosquitto broker project, this lightweight library offers basic MQTT client functionality and is particularly well-suited for applications that require simple and efficient publish-subscribe communication. The Mosquitto client library provides functions for establishing connections, publishing messages, subscribing to topics, and handling incoming data with minimal overhead. It is often chosen for applications that prioritize simplicity and portability, such as embedded systems or IoT devices with severe resource limitations.

For developers working on constrained embedded platforms, the Eclipse Embedded MQTT Client library, sometimes referred to as MQTT-C, provides a minimalistic implementation of MQTT designed specifically for devices with limited memory and processing capabilities. This library is written in ANSI C, ensuring compatibility with virtually any C compiler and embedded platform. It is designed to operate without dynamic memory allocation, making it particularly useful in environments where malloc and free are avoided due to real-time requirements or memory fragmentation concerns. The library is also transport-agnostic, allowing developers to implement custom transport layers such as UART, SPI, or proprietary wireless protocols, in addition to standard TCP/IP stacks.

Energy efficiency is a top priority when implementing MQTT clients in embedded systems. C and C++ MQTT libraries allow fine-grained control over client behavior, enabling developers to minimize network activity and reduce power consumption. Techniques such as tuning keep-alive intervals, batching message publications, and optimizing connection management are easily achievable through the low-level APIs provided by C and C++ libraries. Developers can design clients that wake from low-power sleep modes only when necessary to publish critical data, extending battery life and reducing maintenance frequency in field-deployed devices.

C and C++ MQTT clients are frequently integrated with RTOS environments to create highly responsive and deterministic applications. For example, when using FreeRTOS, developers often build MQTT clients that run within a dedicated task, using the RTOS's scheduler to manage concurrent activities such as sensor reading, data processing, and communication. MQTT libraries designed for C and C++ often include APIs that are safe to use within real-time systems, ensuring predictable timing and minimal resource contention.

In automotive, industrial automation, and medical device sectors, where certification and compliance are often mandatory, the use of C and C++ MQTT libraries provides the transparency and control necessary for meeting rigorous safety standards. The deterministic behavior of statically compiled C code and the ability to inspect every line of the MQTT library's implementation makes it easier for organizations to comply with standards such as ISO 26262 in automotive or IEC 62304 in medical device software.

Debugging and diagnostics are integral to developing robust MQTT clients in C and C++. Developers can leverage low-level logging mechanisms, packet inspection tools, and integrated debugging environments to trace connection issues, monitor message flow, and verify client-broker interactions. Many MQTT libraries include configurable logging facilities, allowing engineers to enable or disable logs at compile-time to reduce runtime overhead in production builds. Combined with tools like Wireshark for capturing MQTT traffic, C and C++ developers gain full visibility into protocol-level behavior, enabling precise optimization and troubleshooting.

C and C++ MQTT clients also integrate seamlessly with legacy systems and other protocols used in industrial and embedded applications, such as Modbus, CAN, or OPC-UA. By acting as protocol bridges, MQTT clients written in C or C++ enable existing infrastructure to publish and subscribe to modern IoT networks, providing a migration path from traditional machine-to-machine protocols to scalable cloud-native architectures.

Ultimately, C and C++ remain indispensable for developing MQTT clients where performance, efficiency, and portability are paramount. Whether running on ultra-low-power microcontrollers, embedded gateways, or mission-critical control systems, C and C++ MQTT libraries provide developers with the flexibility and control needed to build reliable and efficient IoT solutions across a wide spectrum of industries.

MQTT Integration with Node-RED

Node-RED is a powerful, flow-based development tool that enables users to wire together devices, services, and APIs in a highly visual and intuitive way. Originally developed by IBM for IoT applications, Node-RED has grown into one of the most popular platforms for rapid prototyping and deploying automation workflows in both industrial and home environments. A core strength of Node-RED lies in its ability to integrate seamlessly with MQTT, making it an essential tool for developers and system integrators who need to process and route MQTT messages without writing extensive amounts of code. The synergy between MQTT and Node-RED allows developers to build IoT applications, automation solutions, and data processing pipelines quickly and effectively.

MQTT is designed to connect lightweight clients to a broker in a publish-subscribe model, which fits perfectly into Node-RED's visual programming environment. Within Node-RED, MQTT nodes allow users to easily subscribe to MQTT topics, process incoming messages, and publish messages to specific topics on a broker. The MQTT integration is simple to configure, requiring only a few key parameters such as broker address, port, and authentication credentials. This ease of setup empowers even non-programmers to deploy MQTT-powered automation flows, bridging the gap between complex backend systems and edge devices.

Once configured, the MQTT input node in Node-RED listens for messages published to specific topics and triggers connected flows upon receipt of data. For instance, a flow can begin when a temperature sensor publishes a reading to a topic such as home/livingroom/temperature. Node-RED can then process this data using built-in nodes for data transformation, conditional logic, and message routing. From here, developers can forward the data to dashboards, cloud services, databases, or trigger local actions such as turning on a fan or sending a notification to a user's smartphone.

Node-RED's modularity enhances its role as an MQTT client. Beyond the standard MQTT input and output nodes, developers have access to a vast library of additional nodes contributed by the open-source community. These nodes provide integrations with cloud platforms like AWS IoT, Microsoft Azure, and Google Cloud, as well as databases such as MongoDB, InfluxDB, and MySQL. Combining MQTT with these capabilities, Node-RED acts as a data hub that collects MQTT data and forwards it to other systems for storage, analysis, or further automation.

A common use case for MQTT and Node-RED integration is in smart home automation. Devices such as smart lights, thermostats, door sensors, and security cameras often communicate via MQTT. With Node-RED, users can create flows that automate tasks such as turning on lights when motion is detected, adjusting heating based on room occupancy, or sending mobile alerts when a door sensor is triggered. For example, a Node-RED flow could subscribe to an MQTT topic home/entry/motion and, upon detecting motion, publish a new message to home/livingroom/lights to switch on the lights automatically. The logic behind this interaction can be configured in Node-RED using simple drag-and-drop nodes and conditional statements without writing complex scripts.

In industrial IoT settings, Node-RED's ability to process MQTT data in real-time enables developers to build monitoring and control applications. Machine sensors publishing data on production metrics, energy consumption, or equipment status via MQTT can be connected to Node-RED flows that aggregate and visualize the information on dashboards. These dashboards, built using Node-RED's dashboard nodes, allow operators to view critical KPIs such as system uptime, temperature trends, or vibration alerts in a web interface accessible from any device on the network. Additionally, Node-RED flows can implement automated responses to specific conditions. For instance, if a machine publishes an MQTT message indicating overheating, Node-RED can trigger a series of actions such as notifying maintenance personnel, logging the event in a database, and sending commands back to the machinery to slow down or shut off via MQTT.

Node-RED's flexibility with MQTT extends to bridging edge and cloud environments. Edge devices that gather data from sensors and publish to a local MQTT broker can have their data routed by Node-RED to cloud services for long-term storage or advanced analytics. By subscribing to local broker topics and publishing selectively to remote brokers hosted in the cloud, Node-RED enables efficient bandwidth usage and maintains responsiveness for local applications. This architecture is especially useful in environments where devices must function autonomously at the edge while periodically syncing critical data with cloud systems.

Security is a key consideration in MQTT and Node-RED integrations. Node-RED supports encrypted connections to MQTT brokers via TLS, and credentials can be securely managed through Node-RED's environment variables or credential store. This allows Node-RED to authenticate as a client to brokers that enforce strict access controls and encryption policies. Additionally, developers can implement further security measures within Node-RED itself, such as validating incoming MQTT messages for correct payload structures or filtering out unauthorized topics.

Another powerful feature of integrating MQTT with Node-RED is the ability to prototype and test IoT applications quickly. Since Node-RED provides immediate feedback through its debug nodes and logging features, developers can experiment with MQTT topics, payload formats, and automation logic in real-time. This iterative workflow accelerates development cycles and simplifies troubleshooting, as issues related to topic subscriptions, message routing, or payload handling can be identified and resolved visually.

In addition to its role as a message router and automation engine, Node-RED can also act as a lightweight MQTT broker using external modules such as Aedes, which can be installed via Node-RED's node package manager. This allows Node-RED to host MQTT topics and manage subscriptions natively, simplifying deployment in small or localized IoT networks where setting up a dedicated broker might be unnecessary.

Overall, Node-RED's integration with MQTT empowers users to create highly customizable, scalable, and maintainable automation systems. Whether deployed in smart homes, industrial facilities, or research labs, the combination of MQTT's efficient messaging protocol with Node-RED's intuitive visual programming interface offers unparalleled flexibility and productivity. Developers, system integrators, and even hobbyists can build real-time, event-driven workflows that leverage the strengths of both tools to connect devices, services, and users seamlessly across distributed IoT networks.

MQTT and Serverless Architectures

The rise of serverless architectures has transformed how modern applications are designed and deployed, offering scalability, cost-efficiency, and simplified infrastructure management. In serverless models, applications run as discrete functions on managed platforms, abstracting away server provisioning and maintenance tasks from developers. MQTT, with its lightweight and event-driven nature, integrates seamlessly into serverless workflows by acting as a highly efficient data ingestion and distribution mechanism. When paired with serverless computing platforms such as AWS Lambda, Azure Functions, or Google Cloud Functions, MQTT enables developers to build scalable, event-driven IoT solutions that process data in real time and automatically respond to device activity without the need for dedicated servers.

MQTT's publish-subscribe communication model is inherently suited to event-driven applications. Devices such as sensors, actuators, and edge gateways publish messages to an MQTT broker based on system events, environmental readings, or user inputs. Serverless functions can be triggered downstream whenever these MQTT messages arrive, allowing for highly reactive and automated workflows. For instance, when an MQTT broker receives a message from a temperature sensor indicating a sudden spike in heat levels, a serverless function could be triggered to evaluate the data, store it in a database, notify a system operator, or even send control commands back to the field devices via another MQTT publication.

In cloud-native architectures, MQTT brokers often serve as the entry point for IoT device data, collecting messages and forwarding them to serverless platforms for further processing. Managed MQTT brokers such as AWS IoT Core, Azure IoT Hub, or Google Cloud IoT Core make this integration even more seamless. These cloud providers offer built-in rules engines and connectors that automatically route incoming MQTT messages to associated serverless functions without requiring complex custom code. In AWS IoT Core, for example, a rule can be configured to forward MQTT messages directly to an AWS Lambda function, where the data can be processed, validated, or enriched before being routed to other services.

One of the primary advantages of integrating MQTT with serverless architectures is the ability to achieve dynamic scaling. Serverless platforms automatically adjust the number of function instances in response to fluctuating workloads. During periods of high device activity, when hundreds or thousands of MQTT messages are published concurrently, serverless systems can instantly scale up to process all incoming data in parallel. Conversely, during periods of low traffic, serverless platforms reduce the number of running functions to zero, conserving cloud resources and lowering operational costs. This elasticity is especially valuable in IoT systems where device activity is unpredictable and can vary greatly over time.

Another key benefit is the reduction of operational complexity. By offloading the responsibility for infrastructure management to the serverless platform provider, developers can focus on writing application logic rather than managing servers, containers, or orchestration systems. Serverless functions triggered by MQTT messages are typically stateless, short-lived, and self-contained, which simplifies development and deployment processes. Developers can deploy new features or make changes to the processing logic with minimal disruption to the overall system.

In practical terms, integrating MQTT with serverless architectures enables a wide range of IoT applications. In smart agriculture, for example, sensors deployed in fields publish environmental data such as soil moisture, temperature, and humidity to an MQTT broker. Serverless functions can subscribe to these data streams and execute logic to analyze trends, forecast weather patterns, or trigger irrigation systems when necessary. Because serverless functions are event-driven, they remain dormant when no data is received, reducing energy and compute consumption while maintaining the ability to respond instantly to critical events.

In smart building management systems, MQTT-enabled devices such as occupancy sensors, HVAC controllers, and lighting systems publish events that trigger serverless functions to optimize energy usage. When an MQTT message indicates that a conference room is unoccupied, a serverless function can execute automation logic to adjust lighting, reduce air conditioning output, and log the event for future analysis. This approach improves operational efficiency while avoiding the need for dedicated backend servers or complex scheduling systems.

Security plays a critical role in MQTT and serverless integrations. MQTT messages often contain sensitive data, especially in healthcare, manufacturing, or critical infrastructure settings. Cloud providers implementing serverless platforms offer robust security mechanisms such as IAM (Identity and Access Management) roles, policy enforcement, and environment isolation to protect serverless functions. Additionally, TLS encryption is employed to secure MQTT communication channels between devices and brokers. Functions triggered by MQTT events also inherit the security context of the cloud provider's environment, ensuring that data access and modification rights are tightly controlled.

Another compelling aspect of combining MQTT with serverless architectures is the ease of integrating data with other cloud-native services. Once an MQTT message triggers a serverless function, the processed data can be streamed into cloud storage, databases, analytics platforms, or notification services. For example, processed IoT data can be stored in Amazon S3, written to DynamoDB or BigQuery, or forwarded to real-time dashboards for monitoring purposes. Developers can also integrate machine learning services such as AWS SageMaker or Google Vertex AI to enable predictive analytics or anomaly detection workflows within the serverless functions.

Monitoring and observability are also enhanced in serverless MQTT integrations. Most cloud providers offer built-in monitoring tools such as AWS CloudWatch, Azure Monitor, or Google Cloud Operations Suite, allowing developers to track function execution metrics, monitor latency, and detect anomalies in near real-time. Logs from serverless functions can be collected automatically, offering insights into MQTT message handling, error rates, and system performance. These metrics provide valuable feedback to optimize processing logic and ensure that the system continues to operate efficiently under varying load conditions.

Another interesting use case is integrating MQTT and serverless architectures with low-code or no-code platforms. Using services such as AWS Step Functions or Azure Logic Apps, serverless workflows can be visually orchestrated to include MQTT-triggered functions alongside other cloud services. This approach enables rapid development of complex automation workflows without the need for extensive programming, making IoT development more accessible to non-developers or multidisciplinary teams.

Ultimately, MQTT and serverless architectures complement each other perfectly, enabling organizations to create highly scalable, event-driven applications with minimal infrastructure overhead. By harnessing the strengths of both technologies, developers can design agile and resilient IoT ecosystems capable of processing massive data volumes, executing business logic on demand, and delivering real-time insights with minimal latency. Whether supporting smart factories, energy grids, transportation systems, or consumer IoT applications, the combination of MQTT and serverless computing provides a flexible and future-proof foundation for modern connected systems.

MQTT in Multi-Protocol IoT Systems

The Internet of Things (IoT) landscape is inherently diverse, with numerous devices, applications, and systems using different communication protocols based on their specific requirements. In many real-world IoT deployments, a single protocol is insufficient to meet the demands of every component in the system. This is where multi-protocol IoT systems come into play. These systems integrate multiple communication standards such as MQTT, HTTP, CoAP, Zigbee, LoRaWAN, Bluetooth Low Energy (BLE), and Modbus to create a cohesive and interoperable network. Among these protocols, MQTT often plays a pivotal role due to its lightweight nature, scalability, and efficient publish-subscribe model, acting as a bridge or data aggregator between other protocols and higher-level applications.

In multi-protocol environments, MQTT is frequently used as the core backbone for device-to-cloud or device-to-application communication. While edge devices or sensors might use protocols such as Zigbee or BLE for local, low-power mesh networks, the data collected is often forwarded to an MQTT broker via an edge gateway. This gateway serves as a protocol translator, receiving sensor data over short-range protocols and republishing it to an MQTT broker where cloud services, data analytics platforms, or remote management systems can consume it. This architectural approach allows organizations to take advantage of the strengths of various protocols at different layers of the network while maintaining centralized control and visibility through MQTT.

For example, in a smart building deployment, devices such as motion detectors, temperature sensors, and lighting controllers might communicate using Zigbee or Z-Wave within a local mesh network due to their low-power consumption and reliable local coverage. An edge gateway connected to this mesh network can collect messages and convert them into MQTT publications for distribution to cloud services or on-premise building management systems. Through MQTT, building operators gain real-time insights into the state of the facility, control devices remotely, and automate processes such as lighting, HVAC, or access control.

In industrial IoT systems, legacy protocols such as Modbus or OPC-UA are still widely used to connect programmable logic controllers (PLCs), SCADA systems, and factory equipment. These protocols, while effective in industrial settings, were not originally designed for seamless integration with cloud-based platforms. By incorporating MQTT into the architecture, developers can create gateways or middleware services that translate Modbus or OPC-UA messages into MQTT topics, enabling legacy devices to participate in modern IoT ecosystems without replacing existing infrastructure. This approach bridges the gap between traditional industrial systems and contemporary applications, allowing enterprises to modernize operations while preserving valuable assets.

Another common scenario is found in agricultural IoT applications, where long-range protocols such as LoRaWAN are used to connect remote sensors and devices over extended distances in fields or rural areas. LoRaWAN excels in low-bandwidth and low-power communication, but it is not optimized for complex data routing or integration with cloud services. Gateways receiving LoRaWAN payloads often convert them into MQTT messages, enabling seamless integration with cloud-based analytics services, dashboards, and automation platforms. By utilizing MQTT as a central protocol, developers can aggregate data from geographically distributed sensors into a unified messaging system that supports advanced analytics and decision-making processes.

The versatility of MQTT in multi-protocol IoT systems extends to its ability to act as a unifying transport layer for cloud services. Modern IoT ecosystems often involve interactions between multiple cloud platforms, third-party APIs, and microservices. MQTT's lightweight publish-subscribe model enables efficient communication between these distributed components. For example, an application might combine MQTT with HTTP REST APIs to enable cloud-to-cloud integrations, where processed data is forwarded from the MQTT broker to external services for additional processing or visualization.

Edge computing further amplifies MQTT's role in multi-protocol systems. Edge devices, gateways, or fog nodes equipped with MQTT clients and additional protocol stacks can execute real-time data filtering, preprocessing, and protocol conversion locally. This minimizes data transfer to the cloud, reduces latency, and optimizes bandwidth usage. In environments such as smart grids or oil and gas pipelines, where latency and bandwidth constraints are critical, edge computing nodes can use MQTT to manage and route only essential data to cloud services while handling localized processing via other protocols such as Modbus TCP or DNP3.

Security and interoperability are key considerations when integrating MQTT with other protocols. Multi-protocol gateways must ensure secure translation and data integrity between systems with differing authentication methods and transport security levels. For example, while BLE may lack native encryption in some implementations, MQTT messages published to a broker should be secured using TLS. Access control policies need to be enforced consistently across protocol boundaries to prevent unauthorized access to sensitive data or control mechanisms. Developers often implement fine-grained access controls, topic restrictions, and secure key management to ensure end-to-end security in heterogeneous environments.

Message formatting and data models are additional challenges that MQTT helps to address in multi-protocol systems. Different protocols often use distinct payload structures and encoding formats, such as

JSON, CBOR, XML, or proprietary binary formats. Gateways and middleware that bridge these protocols to MQTT typically include data transformation layers that normalize incoming data into standardized formats for MQTT publications. This standardization simplifies the integration with backend systems and analytics platforms, which can subscribe to MQTT topics knowing that message formats are consistent and predictable.

MQTT's retained message feature also plays an important role in bridging systems with different operational patterns. Some legacy devices might only report status information periodically or upon request. By using retained messages, MQTT brokers can store the latest known value of a topic, making it available to subscribers immediately upon subscription. This functionality is valuable when connecting systems that rely on intermittent updates or event-driven communication.

In smart city applications, multi-protocol systems powered by MQTT enable diverse infrastructure components to work together harmoniously. Traffic control systems using wireless mesh networks, parking sensors communicating over cellular networks, and environmental monitoring stations using LoRaWAN can all publish data via MQTT through appropriate gateways. City-wide management platforms can subscribe to these MQTT topics to gain a holistic view of urban infrastructure and implement data-driven policies to enhance transportation efficiency, public safety, and environmental sustainability.

Ultimately, MQTT acts as a unifying force in multi-protocol IoT environments by simplifying communication between disparate systems and enabling data interoperability across a variety of protocols and technologies. Its lightweight design, flexible publish-subscribe model, and compatibility with modern and legacy systems alike make MQTT a central component in achieving seamless integration and operational efficiency in complex IoT deployments. Whether in industrial, agricultural, smart building, or smart city contexts, MQTT facilitates the convergence of multiple communication standards into a cohesive and scalable system architecture.

Emerging Trends in MQTT

As the Internet of Things continues to evolve and expand into new industries and applications, MQTT has remained a core protocol powering this transformation. Originally designed as a lightweight communication standard for constrained devices, MQTT has steadily adapted to meet the growing demands of modern connected systems. Today, several emerging trends are shaping the future of MQTT, driving its evolution and extending its relevance across advanced use cases such as industrial automation, smart cities, healthcare, transportation, and cloud-native applications. These trends include the rise of MQTT 5.0 adoption, tighter integration with edge computing, the growing role of AI and machine learning in MQTT ecosystems, serverless architectures, and the push toward greater standardization and interoperability.

One of the most notable trends is the increasing adoption of MQTT 5.0, the latest version of the protocol. MQTT 5.0 introduces several enhancements over its predecessor, MQTT 3.1.1, aimed at improving scalability, flexibility, and performance. Features such as session expiry intervals, message expiry intervals, topic aliases, and user properties give developers more control over message behavior and metadata management. Additionally, MQTT 5.0 introduces negative acknowledgments, known as reason codes, which provide explicit feedback when subscriptions or publications fail. These new capabilities allow system architects to design more robust and fault-tolerant applications, making MQTT 5.0 particularly attractive for enterprise and industrial environments where operational resilience is paramount.

Another emerging trend is the proliferation of edge computing in MQTT-based deployments. As more organizations move processing closer to data sources, MQTT is increasingly used to facilitate communication between edge devices and local compute resources. Edge brokers deployed in factories, hospitals, smart buildings, or remote sites aggregate and preprocess data locally before forwarding critical information to cloud services. This distributed approach reduces latency, conserves bandwidth, and enhances system resilience by allowing edge nodes to operate autonomously when connectivity to centralized platforms is unavailable. MQTT's lightweight and efficient design make it ideal for constrained edge devices operating on limited processing power or intermittent network links.

The intersection of MQTT with artificial intelligence and machine learning is also gaining momentum. AI-powered applications are now being embedded at the edge, leveraging MQTT as the communication layer for ingesting sensor data and disseminating inference results. Machine learning models trained on historical IoT data can now run locally on edge devices or gateways to detect anomalies, predict failures, and optimize system performance in real time. MQTT's publish-subscribe model allows AI agents to subscribe to relevant data streams and publish actionable insights without introducing significant overhead. This trend is evident in sectors such as predictive maintenance, where vibration or temperature data is collected via MQTT and analyzed at the edge to predict equipment failures before they occur.

Cloud-native MQTT deployments are becoming increasingly common as organizations embrace containerization and microservices to build scalable and resilient applications. MQTT brokers are now being deployed as Docker containers or managed Kubernetes services, enabling seamless scaling and orchestration of MQTT infrastructure across hybrid or multi-cloud environments. Tools such as Kubernetes Operators and Helm charts are frequently used to automate the deployment and management of MQTT brokers like Eclipse Mosquitto, EMQX, and HiveMQ. This cloud-native approach supports elastic scaling, automated failover, and simplified DevOps workflows, making it easier to adapt to changing workloads and expanding device networks.

The integration of MQTT with serverless computing platforms is another trend reshaping modern IoT architectures. Serverless services such as AWS Lambda, Azure Functions, and Google Cloud Functions are increasingly used to process MQTT-triggered events. When MQTT brokers receive messages, serverless functions can be invoked to execute business logic, transform data, or trigger automation workflows without the need to manage dedicated servers. This model offers several benefits, including reduced operational costs, simplified infrastructure management, and instant scalability. As MQTT continues to power event-driven architectures, the synergy with serverless computing is likely to become even more prevalent in the coming years.

Standardization and interoperability are also becoming critical focal points as the IoT ecosystem grows more complex. While MQTT provides a standardized messaging layer, the diversity of payload formats and topic structures across different vendors and applications can lead to fragmentation. Emerging trends point toward greater efforts to define industry-specific data models, topic conventions, and best practices for MQTT usage. Initiatives such as Sparkplug B are addressing this need by defining a unified topic namespace and payload format for MQTT communication in industrial automation. Sparkplug B enhances interoperability between devices, applications, and platforms, simplifying integration efforts and accelerating deployment timelines.

Security is another area of focus as MQTT continues to expand into mission-critical applications. Emerging trends include the increased adoption of mutual TLS authentication, OAuth 2.0 integration, and the use of hardware security modules (HSMs) to manage cryptographic keys securely. With the growth of multi-tenant cloud services and public IoT networks, ensuring the confidentiality, integrity, and authenticity of MQTT messages has become more critical than ever. Organizations are increasingly applying zero-trust principles to MQTT deployments, ensuring that every client, broker, and service is properly authenticated and authorized to access specific resources.

The trend toward data-centric and analytics-driven IoT platforms is driving greater integration of MQTT with big data and stream processing technologies. MQTT is increasingly used to feed data into systems such as Apache Kafka, Apache Flink, and cloud-native data lakes, enabling real-time and batch analytics at scale. By connecting MQTT brokers directly to event streaming platforms, organizations can build end-to-end pipelines that move IoT data from the edge to advanced analytics engines. This enables use cases such as anomaly detection, demand forecasting, and operational optimization, providing deeper insights into system performance and user behavior.

MQTT is also making inroads into vertical-specific solutions beyond traditional IoT. In connected healthcare, MQTT is supporting remote patient monitoring by securely transmitting real-time health data from wearable devices to healthcare providers. In smart transportation, MQTT powers vehicle-to-infrastructure (V2I) and fleet management systems by providing low-latency communication between vehicles, control centers, and cloud platforms. In agriculture, MQTT is facilitating precision farming applications, enabling farmers to monitor soil conditions, weather data, and crop health in real time.

As these trends continue to unfold, MQTT is poised to remain at the center of innovation in IoT and beyond. Its ability to adapt to emerging technologies such as edge AI, serverless computing, and cloud-native infrastructure makes it a versatile and future-proof solution for building modern, connected systems. By embracing these evolving trends, organizations can leverage MQTT not just as a communication protocol but as a strategic enabler of digital transformation, automation, and data-driven decision-making across industries.

Challenges and Pitfalls in MQTT Deployments

While MQTT is widely regarded as a lightweight, flexible, and efficient messaging protocol, deploying it at scale presents several challenges that organizations must carefully navigate to ensure reliable and secure operations. As MQTT is integrated into increasingly complex IoT ecosystems, common pitfalls related to network stability, security, scalability, message reliability, and system monitoring can arise. Understanding these challenges is essential for architects, developers, and system administrators aiming to build resilient and efficient MQTT-based solutions.

One of the primary challenges in MQTT deployments is network instability, especially when operating across distributed or resource-constrained environments. IoT devices that rely on wireless communication protocols such as Wi-Fi, LoRaWAN, or cellular networks often experience variable signal strength, intermittent connectivity, or high packet loss rates. Since MQTT depends on TCP, network disruptions can lead to frequent client disconnections and reconnections, increasing overhead on brokers and degrading system performance. Devices that reconnect repeatedly can also trigger broker-side resource exhaustion, as each connection consumes memory and processing power. Developers must therefore implement robust reconnection strategies and optimize keep-alive intervals to mitigate the impact of unreliable networks on MQTT communication.

Another significant challenge is ensuring scalability in large-scale MQTT deployments. While MQTT itself is designed for lightweight communication, brokers can become overwhelmed when supporting tens or hundreds of thousands of simultaneous client connections or processing high volumes of published messages. Poorly optimized brokers may suffer from performance bottlenecks, such as increased message latency, packet drops, or degraded throughput. To address scalability concerns, architects often need to implement broker clustering, load balancing, and horizontal scaling strategies. However, designing and managing these distributed architectures adds complexity to the system and requires specialized knowledge of load distribution, session persistence, and message routing mechanisms.

Security is another critical concern that is sometimes overlooked in MQTT deployments. MQTT's simplicity means that it does not enforce built-in security features beyond its basic username and password authentication mechanism. Without additional safeguards, MQTT deployments may be vulnerable to unauthorized access, data interception, or denial-of-service attacks. A common pitfall is deploying brokers without enforcing TLS encryption, exposing MQTT messages to potential eavesdropping or tampering, especially on public or untrusted networks. Organizations must implement strong encryption, mutual TLS authentication, and access control lists (ACLs) to restrict which clients can publish or subscribe to specific topics. Failure to secure MQTT deployments properly can result in data breaches or the manipulation of critical system components, particularly in industries like healthcare, transportation, or industrial automation.

Topic structure and naming conventions represent another frequent challenge in MQTT deployments. MQTT's flexible topic hierarchy system allows developers to organize message flows effectively, but poorly designed topic trees can quickly become unmanageable in large systems. Inconsistent topic naming conventions, overlapping wildcards, or overly broad topic subscriptions can lead to inefficient message routing and increased broker resource consumption. For example, a client subscribing to a broad wildcard topic such as sensors/# may receive a flood of irrelevant messages, consuming bandwidth and processing capacity. This issue is exacerbated when combined with retained messages, as new subscribers may receive stale or unnecessary data immediately upon connection. Careful planning of topic hierarchies, coupled with well-defined topic namespaces and filtering logic, is necessary to maintain message clarity and efficiency.

Quality of Service (QoS) levels, while essential for defining delivery guarantees, can also introduce trade-offs and potential pitfalls. QoS o offers fast and lightweight delivery but with no guarantee of message receipt, making it unsuitable for critical commands or status updates. QoS 1 and QoS 2 provide stronger delivery assurances but at the cost of additional overhead due to acknowledgment packets and retries. In high-throughput environments, excessive use of QoS 2 can strain broker resources and increase latency. Some deployments mistakenly apply QoS 2 universally, regardless of the actual criticality of messages, leading to unnecessary network congestion and broker workload. A best practice is to carefully balance QoS selection based on application-specific requirements, reserving higher QoS levels for essential data only.

Session persistence and message retention introduce further complexity. While MQTT supports persistent sessions to store undelivered messages for disconnected clients, improper use of this feature can result in excessive broker memory usage or message backlogs. For example, if a client with a persistent session fails to reconnect within an expected time frame, queued messages can accumulate on the broker indefinitely, consuming valuable resources. Similarly, retained messages intended to store the last known state of a topic can become problematic if published indiscriminately or without proper lifecycle management. Regular audits of persistent sessions and retained messages, along with appropriate session expiry configurations, help prevent resource exhaustion and maintain broker performance.

Monitoring and observability often present additional challenges in MQTT deployments. Due to MQTT's lightweight nature, developers may underestimate the need for comprehensive monitoring tools. Without proper visibility into metrics such as client connection counts, message throughput, dropped packets, and broker resource usage, administrators may struggle to detect issues before they escalate into service outages. A lack of real-time monitoring and alerting can lead to prolonged system downtime or performance degradation. Integrating MQTT brokers with monitoring solutions like Prometheus, Grafana, or cloud-native observability platforms provides critical insights into system health and supports proactive maintenance efforts.

Another pitfall is related to handling message payloads. MQTT is payload-agnostic, meaning it does not enforce any specific data format for messages. While this offers flexibility, it also increases the risk of inconsistent payload structures across different devices or applications. In multi-vendor or multi-team environments, this inconsistency can lead to integration challenges, data parsing errors, or loss of information. Establishing common payload standards, such as JSON schemas, CBOR encoding, or adherence to industry-specific protocols like Sparkplug B, mitigates this risk and facilitates interoperability between system components.

Finally, interoperability challenges can arise when MQTT is deployed within multi-protocol environments. IoT ecosystems often involve communication protocols such as HTTP, CoAP, Modbus, Zigbee, or LoRaWAN operating alongside MQTT. Bridging these protocols to MQTT requires middleware or gateways that handle protocol translation, data normalization, and message routing. However, integrating diverse protocols can introduce latency, additional points of failure, or data loss if the bridging logic is not carefully designed. Ensuring seamless interoperability between protocols while preserving message integrity and delivery guarantees demands careful architectural planning and robust testing.

Ultimately, the successful deployment of MQTT systems hinges on careful consideration of these common challenges and pitfalls. By addressing issues related to network reliability, broker scalability, security, topic management, and monitoring, organizations can leverage MQTT to build efficient, secure, and scalable IoT solutions capable of meeting the demands of modern connected ecosystems.

Future of MQTT and IoT

The future of MQTT and IoT is poised for significant transformation as technological innovation, market demands, and global connectivity trends continue to shape the digital landscape. MQTT has already established itself as a cornerstone protocol for the Internet of Things, providing a reliable, lightweight, and scalable solution for message-oriented communication across distributed systems. However, as IoT ecosystems evolve to include billions of devices, from smart sensors and autonomous vehicles to industrial machinery and intelligent infrastructure, MQTT is expected to play an even more critical role in enabling the next generation of interconnected systems.

One key factor influencing the future of MQTT is the continued expansion of edge computing. As edge computing becomes a foundational component of modern IoT architectures, MQTT is expected to be the glue that binds edge devices with local processing nodes and cloud services. Edge computing enables data to be processed closer to the source, reducing latency and conserving bandwidth by filtering or analyzing information locally before transmitting it to the cloud. MQTT's low-overhead design and publish-subscribe pattern make it the ideal protocol for facilitating this distributed communication model. In the coming years, the convergence of MQTT and edge AI will likely empower edge devices to make autonomous decisions based on real-time data, unlocking new possibilities for smart factories, connected healthcare, and urban automation.

MQTT's importance will also rise as 5G and future wireless technologies become more pervasive. The ultra-low latency, high reliability, and massive device connectivity offered by 5G networks will enable complex IoT systems to scale rapidly and efficiently. MQTT's compatibility with resource-constrained devices and its ability to handle millions of simultaneous client connections will make it a key protocol for powering mission-critical IoT applications in transportation, logistics, healthcare, and emergency services. Real-time vehicle-to-infrastructure communication, drone fleet coordination, and intelligent energy grids will depend on the seamless interaction between MQTT-enabled devices operating across high-speed wireless networks.

Another major trend shaping the future of MQTT is the growing need for interoperability and open standards. As IoT ecosystems become more diverse and fragmented, with devices and systems from different vendors operating under different protocols and architectures, achieving true interoperability is a significant challenge. MQTT is positioned to be a central hub in multi-protocol environments, acting as a bridge between legacy systems and modern IoT platforms. Initiatives such as Sparkplug B are advancing the standardization of MQTT message formats and topic structures to ensure that industrial equipment, automation platforms, and analytics engines can seamlessly exchange data. This will be particularly important in smart manufacturing, where MQTT will continue to help unify SCADA systems, PLCs, and cloud services under a common messaging framework.

Security will remain at the forefront of MQTT's evolution, particularly as cyber threats targeting critical infrastructure and IoT systems increase in both sophistication and frequency. The MQTT community and key stakeholders will continue to focus on enhancing security features, including the wider adoption of MQTT 5.0's advanced authentication mechanisms, robust TLS configurations, and integration with modern identity management solutions such as OAuth 2.0 and zero-trust frameworks. Future implementations of MQTT are likely to include more advanced security tooling, automated threat detection capabilities, and compliance with emerging cybersecurity regulations affecting critical sectors like healthcare, energy, and transportation.

Cloud-native development practices and containerization will also influence how MQTT is deployed and managed in the future. As organizations adopt microservices, serverless architectures, and Kubernetes-based solutions, MQTT brokers will increasingly be deployed as highly scalable, containerized services. This shift will enable organizations to build resilient, auto-scaling messaging infrastructures that can support dynamic workloads and global deployments. MQTT brokers will integrate more deeply with service meshes, API gateways, and cloud-native observability platforms, enhancing their ability to serve as the backbone for distributed, event-driven systems across hybrid and multi-cloud environments.

Artificial intelligence and machine learning will become increasingly intertwined with MQTT-driven IoT ecosystems. As organizations collect more sensor data through MQTT brokers, they will leverage AI models to extract actionable insights and optimize operations. Real-time data streams from MQTT-enabled devices will feed AI-powered analytics pipelines capable of detecting anomalies, predicting failures, and automating responses without human intervention. This combination will be particularly impactful in sectors such as predictive maintenance, where machinery data collected via MQTT will be analyzed by edge or cloud-based AI systems to prevent costly downtime and extend equipment life cycles.

Emerging use cases such as autonomous vehicles, connected robots, and digital twins will also drive innovation in MQTT. Digital twin technology, in particular, will benefit from MQTT's ability to deliver real-time state updates from physical assets to virtual models running in the cloud or at the edge. By continuously synchronizing data between IoT devices and their digital counterparts, organizations will be able to simulate, monitor, and optimize operations with unprecedented accuracy. In autonomous systems, MQTT will enable machines to share situational awareness data, coordinate complex tasks, and respond to environmental changes with minimal latency, contributing to safer and more efficient automation in fields such as logistics, agriculture, and smart infrastructure.

Sustainability goals will further influence the future role of MQTT in IoT. Organizations across industries are increasingly prioritizing energy-efficient designs to reduce the environmental impact of connected devices and networks. MQTT's lightweight design is inherently suited for energy-constrained applications, such as battery-powered sensors and remote IoT devices operating in hard-to-reach locations. Future MQTT deployments will likely incorporate additional energy-saving strategies, such as adaptive QoS settings, edge processing to reduce unnecessary data transmission, and smart scheduling mechanisms that limit device wake cycles and radio usage.

The role of MQTT in smart city development will continue to grow as urban centers adopt advanced IoT systems to improve services, reduce congestion, enhance safety, and minimize environmental impact. MQTT brokers will act as central hubs for integrating diverse systems such as public transportation networks, environmental monitoring stations, smart lighting, and emergency response platforms. The protocol's flexibility will allow city planners to implement scalable, interoperable infrastructures capable of supporting the evolving needs of connected urban environments, from automated traffic control to real-time air quality monitoring.

As IoT ecosystems continue to expand into new sectors, the MQTT protocol will also adapt to support emerging applications such as space exploration, undersea monitoring, and remote environmental research. In these scenarios, the ability to operate in extreme conditions with limited connectivity will be paramount, and MQTT's efficient messaging model will remain an essential tool for maintaining communication between remote sensors, autonomous platforms, and centralized control systems.

The continued evolution of MQTT, driven by technological advancements, market demands, and new applications, signals a future where MQTT will remain a foundational element of IoT systems worldwide. Its ability to adapt to modern requirements while maintaining its original strengths of simplicity, efficiency, and flexibility ensures that MQTT will continue to serve as a critical enabler of connected devices and smart automation in the digital age. As organizations seek to build more intelligent, resilient, and secure systems, MQTT will play an indispensable role in shaping the next generation of the Internet of Things.

Case Studies: Real-World MQTT Implementations

The practical application of MQTT in real-world scenarios spans a wide range of industries, each leveraging the protocol's strengths to solve unique challenges. From industrial automation and smart city development to healthcare and transportation, MQTT has proven to be a highly effective and versatile communication protocol. By examining several real-world case studies, we can gain insight into how organizations around the world are utilizing MQTT to enhance operational efficiency, enable real-time decision-making, and build scalable IoT infrastructures.

One of the most prominent examples of MQTT deployment is in the field of smart manufacturing. A leading automotive manufacturer implemented MQTT to streamline its production processes and monitor critical machinery in real-time. The manufacturer integrated MQTT-enabled sensors across its assembly lines to collect data on machine vibrations, temperature, and performance metrics. These sensors published data to local MQTT brokers at the edge, which processed and filtered the information before forwarding it to a cloud-based analytics platform. This real-time monitoring system allowed engineers to detect early signs of equipment failure, predict maintenance needs, and reduce unplanned downtime. The integration of MQTT with predictive maintenance algorithms enabled the manufacturer to optimize machine utilization and improve production throughput, ultimately resulting in significant cost savings.

In the energy sector, a utility company managing a nationwide smart grid adopted MQTT to facilitate communication between distributed energy resources and its central control center. The grid included renewable energy sources such as solar panels and wind turbines, as well as traditional power generation facilities. Each energy asset was equipped with MQTT clients capable of publishing status updates, power generation data, and fault notifications to MQTT brokers located at regional substations. The brokers then relayed the data to a centralized control system, enabling operators to balance energy loads in real-time and respond quickly to system anomalies. The utility's MQTT-powered infrastructure also supported demand-response initiatives by allowing smart meters and customer-side devices to adjust energy consumption dynamically based on grid conditions. This deployment showcased MQTT's ability to handle complex, distributed systems where real-time data and automation play a critical role in maintaining operational stability and sustainability.

In the healthcare industry, a hospital network implemented MQTT to create a real-time patient monitoring system. The solution involved integrating MQTT-enabled medical devices such as heart rate monitors, infusion pumps, and ventilators with the hospital's central monitoring platform. Each device published patient vitals and equipment status to a secure MQTT broker deployed on-premises. Medical staff subscribed to relevant MQTT topics via desktop and mobile applications, receiving immediate alerts when patient readings exceeded predefined thresholds. The use of MQTT allowed for seamless communication between bedside devices and hospital personnel, reducing response times during critical situations. Furthermore, the MQTT broker was integrated with the hospital's electronic health record system, automatically updating patient charts with vital signs and device logs. This case highlighted how MQTT can enhance patient care, streamline clinical workflows, and ensure data consistency across healthcare applications.

Smart city projects have also adopted MQTT to connect diverse urban infrastructure components. A metropolitan city government implemented MQTT to integrate its traffic management system with various IoT devices deployed across the city. These devices included traffic cameras, vehicle detection sensors, smart traffic lights, and air quality monitors. MQTT brokers served as the central communication hub, enabling devices to publish real-time data to topics organized by location and sensor type. The traffic management platform subscribed to relevant topics to optimize traffic light sequences, detect congestion patterns, and trigger dynamic rerouting messages for connected vehicles. Additionally, air quality data collected from distributed sensors was used to implement pollution control measures, such as adjusting traffic flow or issuing public health alerts. MQTT's lightweight protocol ensured efficient and reliable communication over the city's existing wireless infrastructure, minimizing latency and supporting the city's goal of improving mobility, reducing emissions, and enhancing public safety.

In the field of agriculture, a large-scale farming operation leveraged MQTT to enable precision agriculture techniques and optimize resource usage. The farm deployed MQTT-enabled soil moisture sensors, weather stations, and irrigation systems across multiple fields. Edge gateways collected sensor data and published it to MQTT brokers, where cloud-based applications subscribed to analyze the data and generate actionable insights. Based on real-time soil conditions and weather forecasts, MQTT-powered automation flows triggered irrigation schedules tailored to specific zones within the farm. This system reduced water consumption, prevented over-irrigation, and increased crop yields. The farm also integrated MQTT with drone-based imaging systems that provided aerial insights on crop health, pest infestations, and field variability. The combined use of MQTT and precision agriculture tools allowed the farm to make data-driven decisions that maximized efficiency and minimized environmental impact.

In the transportation sector, a public transit agency deployed MQTT to enhance the operational efficiency of its bus fleet. Each bus was equipped with GPS units, vehicle diagnostics systems, and passenger counting sensors, all connected to an MQTT client. These devices continuously published data to a centralized MQTT broker, providing dispatchers with live updates on bus locations, passenger loads, and mechanical health. Real-time visibility into fleet operations enabled the agency to optimize routing, improve adherence to schedules, and respond quickly to unexpected delays or breakdowns. The agency also integrated MQTT with a mobile application that allowed passengers to track bus arrivals in real time, improving the overall commuter experience. MQTT's lightweight design ensured reliable data transmission over cellular networks, even in areas with limited connectivity.

Another noteworthy case study involves a logistics company that used MQTT to modernize its warehouse management system. The company deployed MQTT-enabled barcode scanners, automated guided vehicles (AGVs), and robotic picking systems throughout its distribution centers. The MQTT broker served as the backbone for coordinating task assignments, inventory updates, and real-time notifications between devices and the warehouse management platform. For example, when a customer order was received, the MQTT broker published task messages to AGVs, directing them to retrieve specific items from storage racks. The system also updated stock levels and provided immediate feedback to human operators and management dashboards. By leveraging MQTT, the logistics company reduced order fulfillment times, improved inventory accuracy, and enhanced warehouse throughput.

Across these diverse case studies, several common themes emerge. MQTT enables real-time data exchange, simplifies integration between heterogeneous devices and systems, and supports scalable architectures capable of handling large numbers of clients and messages. Its low-bandwidth requirements, flexibility, and event-driven model make it a preferred choice for organizations seeking to build resilient and efficient IoT infrastructures. From improving industrial operations and enhancing public services to advancing patient care and optimizing resource usage in agriculture, MQTT has demonstrated its value as a foundational technology in the expanding world of IoT. These real-world implementations provide a glimpse into the transformative potential of MQTT across industries and hint at even broader applications as IoT continues to evolve.

Final Thoughts and Best Practices

As MQTT continues to grow as a foundational protocol within the Internet of Things ecosystem, it is clear that its impact will remain significant in shaping the next generation of connected devices and systems. The success of MQTT lies in its simplicity, flexibility, and adaptability, which has enabled its adoption across industries ranging from smart cities and industrial automation to healthcare, transportation, agriculture, and beyond. While its lightweight publish-subscribe model has made it the go-to solution for low-bandwidth and resource-constrained environments, fully leveraging MQTT requires a thoughtful approach and the application of well-established best practices.

A key consideration when deploying MQTT solutions is understanding the requirements of the specific application and selecting appropriate Quality of Service levels. Many deployments make the mistake of uniformly applying QoS 2, believing it ensures maximum reliability, but this comes at the cost of increased bandwidth usage and broker workload. Instead, system architects should assess the criticality of each message type and assign QoS levels accordingly. For non-critical sensor data or telemetry, QoS 0 may be sufficient to maintain efficiency and reduce overhead. For control messages or alerts where guaranteed delivery is vital, QoS 1 or QoS 2 can be selectively applied to meet reliability standards without overburdening the system.

Security must be treated as a core component of any MQTT-based architecture, not as an afterthought. MQTT itself does not enforce built-in encryption, so it is crucial to implement TLS to protect data in transit, especially in deployments involving public or untrusted networks. Securing broker endpoints with strong TLS configurations, enforcing mutual TLS authentication where possible, and regularly rotating client credentials are all best practices that should be followed. Access control should be fine-grained, using well-structured ACLs to prevent unauthorized clients from subscribing to or publishing on sensitive topics. Furthermore, system administrators should implement intrusion detection and monitoring tools to identify abnormal traffic patterns or unauthorized access attempts.

Proper topic hierarchy design is another vital element of a successful MQTT deployment. A clear and logical topic structure improves system maintainability, message filtering, and routing efficiency. Developers should adhere to naming conventions that reflect device type, location, function, and data type. For instance, a topic such as factory/line1/temperature/sensor5 provides a clear context for the message and enables precise subscriptions. Avoiding overly broad wildcard subscriptions is also recommended, as this can result in excessive traffic to clients that may not need all available data. Organizing topics into meaningful layers ensures that the MQTT system remains scalable and manageable as the number of devices and data streams grows.

Broker selection and deployment strategy are equally important. Whether choosing an open-source broker like Eclipse Mosquitto or EMQX or opting for a commercial solution with advanced features, organizations must ensure that the broker can handle the anticipated load while offering necessary features such as clustering, load balancing, and high availability. In larger deployments, broker clustering and geographic distribution improve resilience and latency while supporting disaster recovery and business continuity plans. It is essential to evaluate broker performance under expected workloads through load testing and to configure monitoring tools that track metrics such as message throughput, connection counts, and resource utilization.

For IoT environments where edge computing plays a role, integrating MQTT brokers at the edge provides significant benefits in terms of responsiveness, reduced latency, and minimized bandwidth consumption. Edge brokers can preprocess or filter data locally, reducing the amount of information sent to cloud platforms while maintaining autonomy during intermittent network disruptions. When combined with lightweight edge AI models, edge brokers can also contribute to localized decision-making, enabling real-time control systems that do not rely on constant cloud connectivity.

Retained messages and persistent sessions are powerful MQTT features but must be used judiciously. Retained messages are helpful for sharing the latest device state with new subscribers, but excessive use or failure to clear outdated retained messages can lead to confusion and resource waste. Similarly, persistent sessions should be configured with appropriate session expiry settings to prevent brokers from storing stale messages for clients that may no longer reconnect. Regular audits of retained messages and persistent session queues ensure that system resources are used efficiently and that data integrity is maintained.

Monitoring and observability are essential for the long-term success of any MQTT deployment. Integrating brokers with monitoring solutions like Prometheus and Grafana enables administrators to visualize system health and performance metrics in real-time. Alerts should be configured for key indicators, such as sudden increases in client disconnections, message drop rates, or CPU and memory spikes on broker nodes. Centralized log aggregation and analysis help detect trends and pinpoint the root causes of issues, facilitating proactive maintenance and minimizing system downtime.

Another critical best practice is ensuring interoperability between MQTT and other protocols in multi-protocol environments. Many IoT systems require interaction between MQTT and technologies such as HTTP, CoAP, Modbus, or LoRaWAN. Well-designed protocol bridges and gateways facilitate seamless data exchange between systems and ensure that legacy devices can integrate with modern MQTT-powered platforms. When bridging between protocols, attention must be paid to data formatting and normalization to ensure consistency and prevent parsing or processing errors downstream.

Finally, fostering a culture of continuous improvement and knowledge sharing within development and operations teams ensures that MQTT deployments remain aligned with evolving project requirements and technological advancements. As MQTT continues to develop, particularly with the growing adoption of MQTT 5.0 and emerging standards like Sparkplug B, teams should stay informed of new features, community best practices, and security recommendations.

The journey from initial design to full-scale deployment of an MQTT system involves careful planning, robust implementation, and ongoing maintenance. Whether powering smart city infrastructures, enabling real-time industrial automation, or supporting connected healthcare ecosystems, MQTT has proven its ability to deliver efficient and scalable communication. By applying best practices in security, topic management, scalability, and observability, organizations can ensure that their MQTT-based IoT solutions remain resilient, secure, and capable of meeting the demands of the rapidly evolving digital landscape. As MQTT continues to evolve alongside IoT, cloud, and edge computing technologies, it will remain a critical tool for building the intelligent, automated systems that define the connected world.